INTELLIGENCE, IQ AND RACE

WHEN, HOW AND WHY THEY

BECAME ASSOCIATED

ANDRE JOSEPH

INTELLIGENCE, IQ AND RACE—WHEN, HOW AND WHY THEY BECAME ASSOCIATED

ANDRE JOSEPH

San Francisco, California
1977

Published By

R & E RESEARCH ASSOCIATES, INC.
4843 Mission Street, San Francisco 94112

Publishers

Robert D. Reed and Adam S. Eterovich

Library of Congress Card Catalog Number

77-081023

I.S.B.N.

0-88247-479-0

Preface

Because of the need to highlight that IQ tests represent only a special kind of measurement instrument: they are really systems of classification of individuals with reference to others, this book was undertaken. This work is needed to show that thus with such classification systems it is impossible to interpret a deficiency reflected by test scores in other than a socio-cultural frame of reference. The racial-ethnic controversy has in the past three or four years become of major concern in scientific-academic-educational settings and much research challenging traditionally held assumptions are being reviewed. As a result of these concerns many "culture specific" tests of intelligence are being devised and standardized in other than the traditional White middle-class community. The intent of this work is to highlight that all "intelligence" tests are not only culturally specific --- but are biased in favor of the particular segment within the larger culture for which they were devised and standardized.

This work is a social psychological, historical and Black perspective dealing with the concerns of intelligence as it relates to race. It differs from other works on <u>Race and IQ</u> in that it is heavily psychological in nature -- tracing the history of the psychological testing movements in intelligence from early philosophical concerns, to Binet (1905), to the Stanford Revision (1916) to the present. The work incorporates both Social and Psychological concerns as they relate to intelligence, and spotlights when, where and (speculates on) why the three distinct concepts -- Intelligence, IQ, and Race -- became associated. The work also deals with Race and the controversies surrounding this often misused hypothetical construct, from a social anthropological frame of reference. Finally, the work is written by a Black author using his own socialization and Black social framework as a means for speculation.

The work is scientific in nature (although it is written in a modified scientific mode). It is written to be used as a supplemental text in courses dealing with Sociology, Anthropology and Psychology as they relate to cultural differences among differing societies. Also, it can be used as a basic readings text in courses dealing with Psychological testing and intelligence. Further, the text is designed to be of interest to the educated lay population in the larger society (housewives, students, airport set, etc.) who are interested with the concerns and controversies which surround the constructs Intelligence, IQ and Race.

It is felt that one should buy, keep and use this text because it offers a fresh new heavily Black biased approach to viewing Intelligence, IQ and Race.

Table of Contents

ACKNOWLEDGMENTS

I wish to express my sincere appreciation to Professor John W. McDavid for his professional guidance and personal friendship throughout my graduate education, and in particular for his great patience and understanding in guiding this study. Also I am indebted to Professors Barbara Payne, Larry Greeson, and Warren Moore for their valuable suggestions and critiques.

I also wish to thank the many students who through their energy and enthusiam in my classes continually inspired me to greater heights.

Finally I wish to acknowledge the inspiration and encouragement I received from my family, and to dedicate this work in memory of my father - Woodrow Joseph.

INTRODUCTION

"Is IQ really a good measure of intelligence, or simply a good predictor of the things that make for success in America?" (Cohen, 1972). This question challenges the very basic assumptions held by researchers as to what IQ scores actually reflect.

"IQ" is a symbolic representation for a mathematical construct (Intelligence Quotient) popularized by Terman in his 1916 revision of the Binet-Simon Scale. It involves calculation of a child's mental age (MA) --- a hypothetical construct which expresses an individual's mental attainment in terms of the number of years it takes an average child to reach the same level. By dividing this MA by the child's chronological age (CA --- the child's age in years and months) and multiplying by 100, the construct IQ is derived. This procedure was originally suggested by Wilhelm Stern in 1914 at the Fifth Congress of Experimental Psychology as an index of brightness expressed from the results of an intelligence test (Stern, 1914; Goodenough, 1949; Zach, 1972). Later the idea of IQ equivalent (Wechsler, 1944) when an MA is not actually computed, but instead a Table of Norms (i.e., comparisons with others) was used to derive an IQ score. More recently IQ has developed into a full blown entity, interpreted as an innate capacity capable of being transmitted through the genes (Jensen, 1969).

IQ scores play a significant role in the school life of all students in the United States, both Black and White. IQ scores may determine whether a child will be tracked for college preparation or vocational school; assigned to the "Blue Bird or Black Bird" reading group; viewed as gifted or dull; classed as deprived or privileged - or even whether the child will be called a success or failure. Determing the fate of children as they often do, as much light as possible should be shed on what IQ tests actually reflect or measure.

Already much research has questioned the comparison of Black and White IQ scores, with many researchers (Clark, 1965; Kennedy, et al, 1963; Eels, et al, 1951; Havighurst and Breese, 1947; Reese and Lipsitt, 1970 suggesting that present standard-ized tests of IQ are biased against the Black culture. As a result of this redirection, new tests of Black IQ are being de-vised and standardized in the Black community.

There exists no single unified Black culture - but many Black cultures, depending on the social, experiential, and financial backgrounds of Blacks. This is merely to say that Black culture is like White culture in America: it is divided along several lines, such as lower-class, middle-class, and upper-class; with each class characterized by different vari-ables, yet overlapping. Thus, simply developing a Black Ghetto IQ Test will not alleviate discrimination against all Blacks.

2

The Black middle-class (in particular) may still be discriminated against by either White-standardized or Black-standardized tests used to measure intelligence.

In fact, IQ tests must also be developed to be "culture-fair" to this Black middle-class --- and, indeed, for each of the different cultural subgroups in our society which we might wish to assess in comparative studies. To assign value judgments on the basis of such comparisons (e.g., deprived cultures, etc.) is both scientifically unsound and morally unethical when those judgments are based on any kind of culturally biased assessment. Each culture and each ethnic group exists as naturally and legitimately as any other. Proper cultural (ethnic) comparisons are impossible when the value norms from either of the cultural units compared are used as a criterion for judging the other.

PURPOSE OF THE STUDY

This study proposes to show that IQ tests represent a special kind of measurement instrument: they are really only <u>systems of classification</u> of individuals with reference to others (Binet, 1905; Pintner, 1931; Edwards, 1971). With this type of classification system, it is impossible to interpret a "deficiency" reflected by the test score as either acquired or congenital (Binet and Simon, 1905; Edwards, 1971). Further, it is suggested that no tests of intelligence have yet been devised to assess properly any inheritable, genetic potential. The thesis that factors which influence intelligence are heritable is based erroneously on measures using inadequately constructed tests --- even despite the cautions of the authors of these tests, that drawing such conclusions from such tests was improper and beyond the scope of the measurement instruments.

The introduction of Black intelligence tests is a significant undertaking, but it should be possible to show that these measures are not valid for the entire Black population in the United States (Joseph, 1975). If intelligence tests are to be used for comparisons between members of different ethnic groups, then equivalent tests of intelligence must be devised and standardized for all subgroups to be compared in the American population. Then (and only then) could value judgments as to superiority or inferiority of particular groups be logically or ethnically acceptable.

DEFINITIONS OF INTELLIGENCE

Of all the terms in psychological literature, intelligence is probably one of the most nebulous. The term, although used frequently, has no consistent consensually acceptable definition (Pintner, 1931; Goodengouh, 1949; Tyler, 1969; Bayley, 1970; Heim, 1970; Reese and Lipsitt, 1970; Edwards, 1971). Many verbal definitions of intelligence have been proposed, but they vary greatly according to the standpoint from which the psychologist views the problem. Although these definitions of intelligence differ greatly, they are not necessarily contradictory (Pintner, 1931). Bayley (1970) concluded that even with extremely varied wording of definitions of intelligence, there are only two principal areas of differences: (a) disagreement over whether intelligence is a general unitary function or a composite of several more or less independent abilities, and (b) whether intelligence is innate, and grows in a child in somewhat the same manner as he grows in stature, or whether mental abilities are learned and thus increase or decrease in accord with the degree of enrichment or impoverishment of the child's environment. Pintner, in 1931, offered a particularly useful summary description of various definitions of intelligence, in four groups: (a) biological, (b) educational, (c) faculty and (d) empirical (Pintner, 1931).

With _biological_ definitions emphasis is placed upon the adjustment or adaptation of the organism to its environment (or to certain aspects of its environment). Intelligence is conceived as the determining factor in the evolutionary process: the more intelligent organisms adjusting to a greater number of environmental changes. Definitions which fall under this category include: (a) Stern's: "Intelligence is a general capacity of an individual consciously to adjust his thinking to new requirements .... General mental adaptability to new problems and conditions of life" (Stern, 1914); (b) Wells': "Intelligence means precisely the property of so recombining our behavior-patterns as to act better in novel situations" (Wells, 1958); (c) Peterson's: "Intelligence seems to be a biological mechanism by which the effects of a complexity of stimuli are brought together and given a somewhat unified effect in behavior" (Peterson, 1921); (d) Edwards' "Intelligence is capacity for variability or versatility of response," (Edwards, 1928); and (e) Burt's intelligence is "innate, general cognitive ability," (Burt, 1955). These biological definitions assume that intelligent organisms have a multiplicity of responses and can respond to a greater number of situations than unintelligent organisms, and that intelligent behavior leads from one thing to another in ever-widening circles, while unintelligent behavior is narrow and restricted, leading to repetition or cessation (Pintner, 1931).

With _educational_ definitions, emphasis is placed on learning ability --- the educability of the individual. Definitions in this category include: (a) Buckingham's: "Intelligence is the

ability to learn" (Buckingham, 1921); (b) Colvin's: "An individual possesses intelligence insofar as he has learned, or can
learn, to adjust himself to his environment," (Colvin, 1921);
and (c) those many psychologists who define intelligence in
terms of a variety of learning and problem-solving behaviors
(either in the laboratory or naturalistic settings) that go
beyond those incorporated into traditional intelligence tests
(Reese and Lipsitt, 1970). It is assumed that the intelligent
individual learns readily and easily, while those for whom learning is difficult are lacking in intelligence. There appears to
be no necessary contradiction between the educational and biological points-of-view as far as definitions: both regard learning
as adjustment or adaptation to various situations (Pintner, 1931).

The faculty definitions of intelligence emphasizes a
faculty or a capacity. Here the definition is in terms of what
intelligence "is" rather than what intelligence "does." An attempt is usually made to delimit or restrict intelligence and set
it off from other powers or faculties of the mind (Pintner, 1931).
These definitions include: (a) Binet's: "Intelligence is judgment or common sense," (Pintner, 1931); (b) Terman's : "an individual is intelligent in proportion as he is able to carry on abstract thinking," (Terman, 1921) --- which makes intelligence
synonymous with abstract thinking (Reese and Lipsitt, 1970);
(c) Haggerty's: "(Intelligence) is a practical concept connot-
ing a group of complex mental processes traditionally defined in
systematic psychologies as sensation, perception, association,
memory, imagination, discrimination, judgment and reasoning,"

7

(Haggerty, 1921); (d) Jensen's: "(Intelligence is best thought of) as a capacity for abstract reasoning and problem solving," (Jensen, 1969); and (e) Wechsler's: "Intelligence is the aggregate or global capacity of the individual to act purposefully, to think rationally and to deal effectively with his environment," (Wechsler, 1944).

The _empirical_ definitions of intelligence place emphasis on the practical results of intelligence. They call attention to the behavioral value of intelligent responses. For example: (a) Thorndike's: "Intelligence in general as the power of good responses from the point of view of truth or fact," (Thorndike, 1921); (b) Ballard's: "Intelligence is the relative general efficiency of minds measured under similar conditions of knowledge, interest, and habituation," (Ballard, 1921); (c) Pintner's: "Intelligence is merely an evaluation of the efficiency of a reaction or group of reactions under specific circumstances," (Pintner, 1926); (d) Boring's: "intelligence is what tests test," (Boring, 1921); and (e) Pieron's: "intelligence does not exist in mental mechanism; it is only an effect, a functional resultant under certain defined conditions, a behavior value" (Pintner, 1931).

An enormous amount of research has been done in an effort to evaluate the relative merit of these definitions as the "best" --- meaning the "correct" --- definition for intelligence (Reese and Lipsitt, 1970). The literature includes studies using each of the various types of definitions for intelligence presented above. Thus, Reese and Lipsitt (1970) stated that there is "no one intelligence, but as many as there are different cultures (and degrees of differences between cultures)."

Of special concern are those definitions from a biological and an educational (learning) point of view. These two positions have been brought to their apex in the controversy over nature-nurture (genetics-environment) as determinants of intelligence. No unequivocal empirical evidence has been generated to substantiate either the genetic theory of intellectual development or the environmental (learning) theory of intellectual development. Yet many researchers and psychologists appear to work under the assumption that one or the other position has already been ascertained "beyond a shadow of a doubt."

This investigation is addressed to the problems which follow from acceptance of these various assumptions as to the nature and determination of intelligence as fact and thus the various solutions based on supposedly empirical research findings when indeed the findings presently available are equivocal and in no way definitive.

HISTORICAL PROSPECTUS

The history of intelligence testing illuminates both causes and possible cures for the current controversy over definitions and origins of intelligence (Pintner, 1931).

Sociological and Psychological Trends

From a sociological point of view, intelligence tests first originated to fulfill a need --- they came to supply a want in society which stemmed from peculiarities in the mental make-up of the feebleminded.

With the rise of Christianity there was a decided change in the attitude of society towards the physically and mentally defective, with all classes of the despised and rejected being cared for in asylums by the church. Before this time "Exposure" of undesirable children was practiced --- eliminating the weaker feebleminded, but sparing those sound in body. The church showed sympathy and pity, but lacked understanding or helpful services to its wards. The insane were presumed to be under the special protection of God, and the ravings of the fool were sometimes taken for devine revelations.

With the Renaissance, Protestantism brought a change in the attitude of society towards the feebleminded and insane:

they ceased to be "special proteges of the Diety" and became
"children of Satan." They were thought to be possessed of devils
and it was believed that strenuous treatment was necessary to
drive out these demons. Actions of the feebleminded and insane
were now seen as done intentionally of their own will and therefore mental defectives were chastised for their misdeeds.

Around the nineteenth century a more scientific interest
in the insane and feebleminded developed. An era of enlightened
care and definite study of the feebleminded was undertaken by
physicians and psychologists. Early institutions were set up for
the deaf in Paris about 1712 (The Institution for Deaf Mutes
founded by the Abbe de l'Epee, 1712-1789) when it was noted that
such children showed signs of intelligence much above that of the
idiot. The Wild Boy of Aveyron (Juvenis Averionesis, 1797) cre-
ated wider interest in the scientific education of the feebleminded. Itard, a philosophically minded physician of the Institution for Deaf-Mutes undertook to work with the Wild Boy, but
when it dawned on him that the boy was simply an imbecile or
idiot he gave up in despair (Pintner, 1931). The belief of the
time was that idiocy was incurable. Seguin, a student of Itard,
in 1837 undertook the training of a few cases of feebleminded
children and in 1842 convinced Parisian authorities of the desira-
bility of educating the idiots and imbeciles at the Bicetre ---
the beginning of state schools for the feebleminded. Seguin wrote
the first book to deal directly with education and treatment of
the feebleminded, Traitement Moral, Hygiene et Education des
Idiots, 1846. He moved to the United States in 1848, awakening an

11

interest in the treatment of the feebleminded, and in 1864 published <u>Idiocy: Its Diagnosis and Treatment by the Physiological Method</u>. Interest in the treatment of the feebleminded was at the same time well underway in France, England, Germany and Switzerland. The first state institutions for the feebleminded in America were opened in Massachusetts in 1849 and in New York in 1851.

Special classes (rather than schools) were a direct offshoot of this early movement. The backward and dull children were segregated into special classes in the public schools with the idea of stimulating them in order to put them back into the regular classes. This same rationale was used for the segregation of Black and White students in the schools. The first such special class was started in Halle, Germany, in 1859. The idea was soon abandoned when the classes became filled up with feebleminded children who had no possible chance of catching up to the regular classes (Pintner, 1931). In the United States the first special class for backward children appears to have been organized in Cleveland in 1893 (Mitchel, 1929). By the first decade of the twentieth century the special class had become a common feature of the ordinary public school in America.

With this growing interest during the nineteenth century on the part of social reformers and educators in the care of the feebleminded an interest on the part of psychologists appears to have awakened. The first Psychological Clinic in America was opened at the University of Pennsylvania in 1896 under the direction of Dr. Lightner Witmer. The emphasis being on "a careful psychological diagnosis of the nature of the mental deficiency together with an attempt to treat such deficiency as far as it may be amendable to treatment" (Witmer, 1930).

It is in light of these historical sociological trends that Alfred Binet in 1905 developed his tests of mental abilities in order to differentiate which children in the Paris schools were retarded and in need of special education (Zach, 1972).

In America, at the beginning of the twentieth century, interest in individual differences aroused a focus on the possibility of the measurement of intelligence. Cattell (1890-96) at Columbia College tested students during their first and fourth academic years. Cattell fixed the term "test" as denoting a simple task to be performed by subjects in the investigation of individual differences (Pintner, 1931). In "Mental Tests and Measurement," Cattell urged the establishment of norms and standardization of procedures for testing. Bolton (1892) studied the growth of memory and compared results with the intellectual acuteness of the children. Gilbert (1893) gave age norms on 1200 children for a battery of eight tests and showed how scores increased up to puberty; he further compared the test results with teacher's estimates of the pupils' general ability. Johnson, under the influence of the Child Study Movement stimulated by Stanley Hall, compared performance of feebleminded and normal children, although he had no adequate norms for normal children (Pintner, 1931). Ebbinghaus (1897) explored the problem of mental fatigue with his completion tests. Even before the publication of the Binet-Simon Scale in 1905, direct influences of Binet could be

seen. Sharp's work (1899) in the application of certain tests
in memory, imagery, imagination, and attention, etc., was a sample
of this early influence of Binet in America. Kelly's article on
"Psychophysical Tests of Normal and Abnormal Children," (1903)
stated as its purpose --- the attempt to find a simple method of
differentiating between normal and abnormal children. Probably
the most significant work in this country before Binet's Scale
was Norsworthy's assessment of feebleminded children (Pintner,
1931). She gave group tests of intelligence and expressed the
standing of the child in terms of the variability of the group.

These representative studies of individual differences in
American psychology at the beginning of the twentieth century
point out the great interest in the measurement of intelligence.

About the same time in England, Sir Francis Galton was
fostering the Eugenic Movement. His book, Hereditary Genius
(1896) began with this statement: "I propose to show in this
book that a man's natural abilities are derived by inheritance,
under exactly the same limitations as are the form and physical
features of the whole organic world." His emphasis on natural
abilities (which later came to be known as mental traits) as inherited could not for long hold the attention of scientists without raising questions about methods of evaluating of measuring
the abilities that might be inherited. Even in his first book,
Galton constructed an imaginary scale for the measurement of general ability, based on the theory of a normal distribution and
ranged from the lowest idiot to the highest geniuses. "People
differ from each other in general ability by measurable amounts

and cannot be grouped into several distinct and specific types,"
Galton said --- thus tearing down the commonly accepted idea of
the existence of specific types, such as idiots and geniuses
(Galton, 1896).

Galton assumed (without empirical objective tests) that
races varied in intelligence, and he suggested that "negroes might
be as much as two grades below whites." He considered the highest
group to be the Athenians of classical times and he placed them
two grades above modern Europeans.

Galton's idea of general intelligence certainly had tremendous influence on American psychological thought.

BINET - EARLY WORKS

Alfred Binet, born in Nice, France on July 11, 1857 received a law degree in 1878. He studied medicine and worked under Charcot, who probably interested and taught him much in the area of abnormal psychology. He interested himself in the area of psychology during the twenty years between 1878-1898. In 1900, already the founder of L'Annee Psychologique, with many articles to his credit, Binet was given the leadership of the Societe Libre pour l'Etude Psychologique de l'Enfant --- an association of psychologists and school teachers who worked on practical problems in the schools. In 1904, the Minister of Public Instruction appointed Binet a member of a commission (made up of medical men, educators and scientists) to formulate recommendations for the administration of special classes in the public schools of Paris. With Simon, Binet put experimental tests to practical use. Thus appeared their first rough scale in 1905.

The assumption generally held by most psychologists before Binet was that discrimination in sensorimotor tasks reflected intellectual differences (Edwards, 1971). Thus most psychologists used sensorimotor tasks to measure individual differences (Galton, 1894, 1907, 1914; Edwards, 1971). Binet and Henri (1896) rejected

16

this assumption on the basis of empirical observations, stating that an individual may be slow in reaction time relative to discrete sensory motor stimulation, but not necessarily slow in other forms of behavior (Edwards, 1971). Thus it was argued that sensory tests may offer precision but they may not be generalizable to other more general forms of behavior. Some other measurement device was clearly needed (Binet and Henri, 1896; Edwards, 1971).

Binet and Henri were concerned with the question of "what type of measurement would best discriminate between two individuals in intellectual behavior?" They answered by saying that a measurement of complex mental functions would certainly do so. Binet concluded that these complex processes are not readily available to measurement, and many of them are not known. Yet there are such a great number of processes and such great differences between individuals, they felt that imprecision in measurement would nevertheless be tolerable. A new assumption in determining intellectual differences was thus founded; this still underlies most of modern testing procedures. If a significantly large number of superior, complex mental functions are demonstrated by the individual, that number is expected to be large enough to negate imprecision in measurement instruments, in view of relatively great differences between individuals. This assumption is subject to more critical question than it has usually generated. It has apparently been accepted blindly --- in the sense that methodological procedures and item content suggested by Binet and Henri have been used as predominant models in the mental testing movement (Edwards, 1971).

The question then arises as to whether, in fact, differences between individuals in complex mental faculties are sufficiently large, that crude, gross measurements of their effects adequately or accurately reflect such differences. Yet the testing movement appears to have accepted this premise without question.

But there are still other serious questions about Binet's theory of measurement. If one is going to use some results of superior, complex mental functions to reflect individual differences intellectually, how many such functions are there? If there are many of these functions, which ones should be measured? Binet and Henri (1896) avoided these problems by saying that the testing of all functions (even superior ones) in which individuals differ was not necessary. Instead, one should select functions which are representative and significant of the differences between persons (Edwards, 1971). Binet and Henri then also outlined several possible functions to be included in a measurement of mental functions: (a) Memory - a complex function, having expression in a large number of partial memories, (an outgrowth of studies by Charcot and others). Any test of memory function, they said, must sample as many types of memories as possible; with the assumption that the lower the intellectual level of the examinee, the less competent the memory function; (b) Imagery - the commonly held assumption that mental content contains some clear and distinct images; with the kinds, extent, and possible clarity of images being a function of intelligence; (c) Imagination - some unique, indi-

vidual use of experience. It is assumed that the quality of imagination, particularly, should differ among individuals of different intellectual levels; (d) Attention - the essential nature
of attention in intelligent behavior was unknown to Binet
(Edwards, 1971) but he considered it of great significance and
included it as one of the mental functions to be tested; (e)
Comprehension - utilization of several forms of expression, re-
quiring complex tasks for its manifestation; (f) Suggestibility -
ease (or difficulty) with which one is able to be persuaded to
take positions at variance with reality; (g) Aesthetic Appreciation - development of an artistic expression and temperament;
(h) Moral Sentiments - difficult to define or defend (Edwards,
1971) but considered by Binet and Henri a significant enough
variable to be included; (i) Muscular Force (will power) - a
measurement of motor skills which also reflects persistance in a
task even when it becomes uncomfortable; and (j) Motor Skills -
sensorimotor tasks commonly used at the time as measures of individual differences.

How or why these particular measures were chosen was not
made clear by Binet and Henri. However, it should be noted that
the variables recommended by Binet and Henri in 1896 have had
significant impact on the types of variables included in tests of
intelligence presently most widely used in the American schools
(e.g., Stanford-Binet, Weschler, Otis, etc.). Binet and Henri did,
however, recognize problems with using such variables exclusively
and advocated the need for substitutions, changes, and expansions
in the suggested list (Binet and Henri, 1896; Edwards, 1971).

Binet and Henri also suggested the possible combination of tests which might reflect general ability without regard to specific abilities contained in the total test.

It is both unfair and inaccurate to attribute to Binet any statement --- or even assumption --- that his test measured any genetic trait of individuals. He has stated clearly that the content of complex mental functions would differ for persons of different backgrounds and intellectual levels (Binet and Henri, 1896; Edwards, 1971). In fact Binet and Henri advocated that different tests are needed to reflect such differences. Among possible solutions to the charge by Binet that different tests would be needed are these: (a) either a battery of tests of different types and content could be used, according to characteristics of the specific persons to be tested, or (b) a variety of items ranging from simple to complex and reflecting a relatively large number of mental processes might be included within the same test. Binet, and others in the decades following his first scale, reflected the latter viewpoint. Nevertheless, it is not necessarily warranted to conclude that Binet thought this latter position was the best way to measure intellect when comparing persons from differing backgrounds. Binet was interested only in developing an estimate of the intellectual status of a school-age child, such that his educability could be determined. This was for a population which Binet believed to be homogeneous in backgrounds (children in the Paris schools).

Binet and Simon (1905), in publishing their first scale in 1905, cautioned that their purpose was to judge whether a child is retarded or of normal intelligence. Under such conditions they sought to devise a measure of the intellectual level of the child. They held that the sole determinant of mental abilities as measured by their scale should be the child's current intellectual functioning --- not his past history. "Deficiency should be considered in its present scope and form, without attempts to define it as acquired or congenital" (Binet and Simon, 1905). Brain pathology, its determination and extent, was not a matter of concern in the test which they were proposing as a measure of mental abilities. Personality abnormalities were not regarded as suitable for such testings, and persons suffering from these were not to be included. As with historical antecedents, prognosis must also be ignored. Curability or amelioration of a deficiency disclosed by test performance is neither wise nor possible, they felt (Edwards, 1971). Wilhelm Stern (who suggested the use of IQ as an index of intellectual functioning) like Binet, never claimed that the test measured inborn capacity. In 1914, he wrote, "No series of tests, however, skillfully selected it may be, does reach the innate intellectual endowment, stripped of all complications, but rather this endowment, in conjunction with all influences to which the examinee has been subjected up to the moment of testing." (Stern, 1914; Zach, 1972). Thus Binet and Simon in their presentation of the first scale of mental abilities cautioned that this was not <u>measurement</u> in the physical sense, but <u>classification</u> of individuals with reference to others (Pintner, 1931). Such a scale does not measure directly the quality of intelligence, says Binet and Simon (1896). Intellectual qualities may not be placed on a metrical scale in the way that physical qualities can and thus this comparison should be based solely on current intellectual functioning and not on past history acquired or congenital (Edwards, 1971).

THE BINET SCALES

The 1905 Scale

The first scale of Binet and Simon published in 1905 was concerned with a combination of faculties that was later termed general intelligence. Edwards (1971) has stated that specifically, it was differences in the amount of general ability among mentally defective individuals which was the basis for the 1905 scale. Binet and Simon wanted an indication of the intellectual level at which the child was currently functioning. Once this level was determined, comparisons could be made with the level of normal children of the same chronological age, or with children of the same level but varing in age. Although mental age was not utilized in the first scale there were signs of its possible inclusion --- in theory if nothing more. Later in the 1908 scale the concept of mental age was employed.

Binet and Simon cautioned that since the scale was designed to assess educability of school children (Goodenough, 1949; Edwards, 1971; Zach, 1972) the school then is the setting in which intellectual differences must be reflected and measured. Edwards (1971) further stresses these limitations of the original purpose of the scale --- limitations which have been retained to the present day. Binet and Simon stated that what is obtained from the scale is a type of <u>classification</u>; with the performance on the tasks being placed in a hierarchy of performances (Goodenough, 1949; Edwards, 1971). After having determined the performance of two students, comparisons may be made between the two. Further comparisons may be made between normal and subnormal students. Criticism of this first scale has been made in that normal was derived by taking a sample of fifty students selected by teachers as being of normal intelligence. Thus normality in the scale includes a heavy emphasis on average school achievement (Goodenough, 1949; Edwards, 1971).

This scale differed from other scales previously constructed in a number of ways: (1) It made no pretense of measuring any single type of ability or faculty in a precise and adequate manner, but aimed instead at getting a general idea of the child's mental development along as many different lines as possible by setting him a wide variety of tasks; (b) It required only a short time for its administration; (c) The test items were selected with a reasonably clear (and definitely molar) idea of the nature of intelligence: that there were numerous mental processes which comprises intelligence - but that it was not necessary to attempt to measure all of them. Rather, measuring those which were essential factors of intelligence - the ability to make sound judgments; (d) Instead of putting memory tests in one group, numerical problems in another group, the authors arranged the tasks in order of difficulty without regard to their apparent similarity or dissimilarity (Goodenough, 1949).

24

The first scale included thirty specific tasks: (1)
Visual Coordination, (2) Prehension Provoked Tactually, (3)
Prehension Provoked Visually, (4) Cognizance of Food, (5) Seek-
ing Food under Difficulty, (6) Execution of Simple Orders, (7)
Cognizing Objects by Name, (8) Cognizing Pictured Objects by
Name, (9) Naming Objects Designated in a Picture, (10) Compari-
son of Supraliminally different lines, (11) Auditory Memory for
three Digits, (12) Comparison of Supraliminally Different Weights,
(13) Suggestibility, (14) Definition of Familiar Objects, (15)
Memory for Sentences, (16) Differences Between Familiar Objects
Recalled in Memory, (17) Memory for Pictures, (18) Drawing From
Memory, (19) Auditory Memory for more than three Digits, (20)
Resemblances Between Familiar Objects Recalled in Memory, (21)
Discrimination of Lines, (22) Arrangement of five Weights, (23)
Detection of the Missing Weights, (24) Rhymes, (25) Missing Words,
(26) Sentence-Building, (27) Replies to Problem Questions, (28)
Interchange of the Clock Hands, (29) Drawing From a Design cut in
a Quarto-folded Paper, and (30) Distinction Between Abstract Terms
(Whipple, 1910).

The terms on the scale were purported to be arranged in
an order of increasing difficulty - but time proved the need to
make relative modifications. From the scaling, Binet and Simon
felt reasonably sure that an objective classification of degrees
of retardation was feasible. They thus denoted three categories:
(a) Idiocy - the lowest grade of mental deficiency; assigned to
the absence of language. Thus a child of any age who showed an
absence of language - using abstract terms for objects not

physically present, was termed an idiot. An idiot was seen as capable of "parroting" sounds but not able to use these sounds to communicate meaningfully with another person. On the test, an idiot would succeed through item six (execution of simple orders and imitation of gestures). However, items seven (Cognizing real objects by name) and eight (Cognizing objects in a picture by name) would not be passed. An idiot then resembles in performance the normal child of two years or less (Edwards, 1971); (b) Imbecility - the child so designated would not only succeed with items one through six, but with verbal material up through item seven (differences between familiar objects recalled in memory). The imbecile thus shows some degree of verbal functioning, and overall corresponds to the normal child between the ages of two and five (Edwards, 1971); (c) Moronity - the imbecile is most readily distinguished from the moron by performance on task twenty-two (arrangement of five weights) and the portion of task nineteen (auditory memory for more than three digits) where six or more digits comprise the sequence. Otherwise the distinction between imbeciles and morons is not so clear as that between idiots and imbeciles. On some memory tasks the differences between the two are too small to be conclusive (number seventeen, Memory for pictures; number eighteen, drawing from memory, and number twenty-one, discrimination of lines - Edwards, 1971). Criticisms were made that either the tasks were not correctly ordered, or the behavior sampled by the items was not clearly perceptible with the item content, or both.

These children whose behavior was explicitly interpreted to define idiocy and imbecility were in a state institution and there was little difficulty in discriminating between them. However, the children labeled moron were taken from the schools and even then there were difficulties in discriminating between these and normal children, those who could not be successful in the formal program and needed special instructional modes (Goodenough, 1949). Since the purpose of the scale was to make objective and precise distinctions between these two groups (Goodenough, 1949; Edwards, 1971; Zach, 1972) a look into the method employed by Binet and Simon is necessary.

The first step taken was to establish a pool of retarded children of different ages so that appropriate norms might be set up. A list of children between ages eight and thirteen was used to define the subgroup to be studied. School marks of each child were compared to the child's age, so that the oldest children in any class with the lowest marks were singled out (this was the essential method of identifying morons). This is an operational definition with significant consequences (not only for the user of the scale at that time, but also for future users as well). Many researchers have pointed out the need to reemphasize continuously that the Binet method was employed for predicting academic achievement (Binet and Simon, 1905; Goodenough, 1949; Edwards, 1971; Zach, 1972). The children identified by this procedure were included among a group of normal children, and the examiners were not told which children were which. The purpose of the test was to distinguish between the two levels of intellect.

The results indicated that Binet's test did indeed distinguish between the academically successful child and the academically successful child and the academically slow one. With the tasks employing abstract, verbal abilities being the ones which distinguished best between the two groups. Binet and Simon concluded that the moron probably does not develop beyond the level of the average child of twelve (Goodenough, 1949). However, this ceiling does not apply for adult morons since it was assumed that adult morons would have had sufficient experience to perform on abstractions like children above the age of twelve. Peterson (1925) indicated that Binet and Simon assumed these limits either from data collected with eleven-year-olds, or from data simply not reported.

The importance of age comparisons in the use of the scale was undoubted. Binet and Simon reported that no evidence of mental retardation was possible without consideration of age. Implicitly, the degree of retardation depends upon the difference between a child's chronological age and the chronological age of the normal child whom he most resembles. The 1905 scale did not provide for the possibility of determining if a child was above-average, average, or below-average. But the suggestion was there, and it was implemented into the 1908 Scale.

The 1908 Scale

Limitations in the 1905 scale, evidence from Binet's own work, and the work reported by Decrolyn and Degand (1906) led to refinements which were pbulished in 1908. Criticisms accusing

28

Binet and Simon of neglecting theory for the sake of an a priori method only, prompted them to introduce the 1908 scale in which the underlying theory was better explained. Binet again stressed that essentially, the central use of the measure was still to be in the schools, with both normal and abnormal intellectual development the point of concern (Edwards, 1971).

There were two purposes for the work as reported in the paper of Binet and Simon (1908): (1) the determination of the "law" of intellectual development in children through the use of a means for measuring intelligence, and (2) the study of variability in intellectual aptitudes. The first purpose Binet, et al attempted. However, their standardization procedures (which was not mentioned), the sample size (300 Parisian school children within two months of their birthdays from ages three through twelve) and how the sample was selected (not mentioned) --- all are open to criticism. Edwards (1971) felt that the scale certainly measures something, but under the circumstances the pragmatic position would be that the scale measured performance differences allied to school achievement. The second purpose Binet and Simon admitted they did not get a chance to research (Binet and Simon, 1908; Edwards, 1971).

The 1908 Scale is said to be more than a revision of the 1905 scale (Goodenough, 1949; Edwards, 1971). It is a refinement of the 1905 scale with considerable additions and deletions of items based upon empirical evidence. The major differences being that the mental age is now expressed as the score which is obtained and instead of being arranged in order of difficulty, the tests were now grouped according to the age at which they were commonly passed. While the 1905 scale was designed, primarily, to show that a measurement which illustrated individual differences in complex mental processes was possible, the 1908 scale tried to demonstrate the extent to which such differences exist (Goodenough, 1949; Edwards, 1971). Another major difference between the 1905 and 1908 scales was the omission from the latter of the tests designed for use with idiots. Many imperfections of the 1908 scale were found "but however imperfectly it was worked out at this time, the idea was a notable one destined to change the course of mental testing for many years to come." (Goodenough, 1949).

Binet and Simon believed that the results of the test could be used to help determine when and what kinds of instruction should be given to all children (in the Paris schools). Knowing the mental age of a child as determined by this test could be useful in terms of determining when a child was ready to learn a particular topic, for to teach before mental maturity is reached was only a waste of instruction time (Binet and Simon, 1908). Thus the scale would not only have applicability for the child who makes normal progress in school but for determining those of inferior ability and who should have specialized kinds of instructional procedures.

The 1911 Scale

The 1911 Scale (revised shortly before Binet's death) is said to differ in details more than in its major principles

(Goodenough, 1949). A few new items were added, but the majority of items were taken from the 1908 scale and a few items from the 1905 scale. The method of scoring was the same as in the 1908 scale except that a basal age concept was added, thus permitting the use of fractional parts of a year in computing the mental age. Edwards stated that Binet himself was doubtful as to whether the instrument was sufficiently delicate to warrant such a refinement in its use (Edwards, 1971).

Thus nowhere can a systematic mode which might be used and labeled as Binet's theory of intelligence be found (Edwards, 1971). However, gleaning from his writings it would appear that Binet believed that sensorimotor measures would not offer reliable information about intellectual competence because the behavior required was too far removed from the trait to be measured. Instead he recommended assessment of higher complex processes which are not specifically defined. Further, Binet says that it would be difficult to try and classify particular kinds of items as measures of whatever traits are assumed to be higher complex processes (attention, judgment, comprehension, etc.) because all of these forms, to some degree, enter any higher mental operation. Binet concluded that until some specific traits which are significant of complex processes can be defined and measured, some general measure of intelligence would seem to be the preferred one, since it would reflect to some degree all of these at work. Thus he developed what he called scales of general mental abilities. Nowhere did Binet mention the use of his test as a means of determining the etiological, acquired or congenital determinants of intelligence;

31

in fact, Binet cautioned against making such uses of his test in a 1905 article, saying that "deficiency should be considered in its present scope and form," only.

VALIDITY AND RELIABILITY OF THE BINET SCALES

Validity, which refers to the effectiveness of the test
in representing, describing or predicting the attribute that the
user is interested in (Thorndike and Hagen, 1969) or the extent
to which the test measures what it purports to measure, should be
taken into account to ascertain what in essence the Binet Scale(s)
measure.

Because of some early critiques and criticisms of both the
1905 and 1908 scales by Decrolyn and Degand (1910) as a result of
the use of the Binet scale in a private school they operated in
Belgium; Binet had to examine the validity of his scale. One of
the major criticisms of Decrolyn and Degand was that the test
tended to be too easy for young children and too difficult for
older ones, indicating some bias in the scale that was over esti-
mating the abilities of young children, and underestimating those
of older children. This would lead to the conclusion that intelligence declines with age. But Binet and Simon analyzed the data
presented by Decrolyn and Degand, and found that the Belgian
children used as subjects were not of the same social class of
those upon whom the test had been standardized. "Since the
Belgian children were from a private school they tended to be of
a superior social class," and also tended to be (on the average)

about one and one-half years accelerated over the norm. Because of the possibility then existing that social class might be a significant factor in the use of the scale, Binet began a systematic study of differences among social classes in performance on the 1908 scale. In studies done in Paris with children of superior social classes, Binet and several of his colleagues found approximately the same accerleration as had been found with the Belgian children. Those children (Belgian and French) of the superior social class did better on the subtest where language and home training were the most important. Least differences were found in terms of formal academic training (Edwards, 1971). These findings suggest that the tests were not valid for making comparisons between different social levels --- but only within the same social level. Binet, however, never attempted to incorporate into his scale items that would have made for comparisons between social levels (this possibly being due to his death in 1911). Instead Binet's suggestion would probably again be that "different tests would be needed to reflect accurately and appropriately such differences between persons of different backgrounds," as advocated in his article with Henri of 1896. Other researchers, Scheffield (Johnston, 1910, 1911) in England; Goddard (1911) and Terman and Childs (1912) in the United States, and Bobertag (1911) in Germany also confirmed the findings, however, were too late to influence work on the 1911 scale (Edwards, 1971). Stern (1914) and Peterson (1925) however, saw this kind of international agreement as the strongest evidence of the validity of the Binet method for measuring intellectual differences.

Binet and Simon took several other precautions to insure validity of the 1908 scale. They had teachers identify those children who were superior in ability, in terms of classroom achievement. In each instance this was done they found that the child also tended to be above his age norms in the test performance. Contrasting this they took fourteen children who were classified as retarded by three years in academic achievement and found that they also were found on the test performance to be two and a half years mentally retarded, on the average; with the actual range being from one to six years of absolute retardation on the scale (Edwards, 1971). Further studies on the validity of the 1911 scale saw Binet and Simon testing ninety-seven children who were within two months of their birthdays. They were, however, placed in grades which were equivalent to their ages. Binet and Simon computed the deviation of the grade of each child from the school-grade average for his age, as well as the difference of his mental age from his actual age. Differences were then taken between these two scores. On the average, there was only 0.7 years difference between the two scores. Binet and Simon further constructed a table of correlation coefficients which showed high correlation (though not perfect) between academic placement and mental level of each child. Binet and Simon felt that this evidence too supported the validity of the scale (Edwards, 1971). From the above methods one would wonder what in essence Binet was ascertaining the validity of. It would appear that if his scale was valid --- then its validity was defined in terms of the assumption that the score on the test was a measure of classroom achievement. Edwards (1971) stated that the primary use of the scales was to be in the public school settings; for this reason, he states validity must be considered in terms of teacher utilization and teacher judgment about intellectual level.

From the history of the Binet Scales and his own writings Binet appears to profess: that his test was for the most part a measure of school related abilities and should not be generalized out of that context (Binet and Simon, 1905; Goodenough, 1949; Edwards, 1971).

In the 1911 Scale, Binet for the first time became concerned about some kinds of measures of reliability (Edwards, 1971). By the term reliability, Binet seemed to have meant consistency in the way that a child would perform from one testing to the next testing on the scale. Others (Thorndike and Hagan, 1969) have defined reliability in a similar manner: the accuracy or percision with which a measure based on one sample of test tasks at one point in time represents performance based on a different sample of the same kind of tasks or a different point of time or both. Binet had already proposed one means by which such reliability information could be obtained --- take a group of individuals, test them at one time, then fifteen days later retest the same children with the same test. Binet believed, however, that some difference should be obtained in the scores. Peterson (1925) reports a study done in 1910 by a colleague of Binet to determine whether or not such gains did occur. Five children were tested with a fourteen-day interval before retesting. Gains equal to five months were obtained. Binet was so concerned by such a large

36

gain over a two-week period that he left out the items on which gains occurred in his 1911 revision (Edwards, 1971). Binet further pointed out that even a fifteen day interval might be too short and said that intervals of up to a year might not show such gains.

Although a given test may be both reliable and valid when used with a group of subjects for whom the test is appropriate, the same test may be neither reliable nor valid when applied to a group of a different composition (Goodenough, 1949). When a test is given to persons who were not a part of the original standardization group it must be assumed that such persons are sufficiently similar to that group in respect to experience to justify the assumption that they form a part of the same "universe." For whether we are aware of it or not, such an assumption is implicit in every application of a given test to an individual or to a group (Goodenough, 1949).

Binet seems to have been aware of such limitations of the validity of his scale, as it pertains to differences in social classes and environmental backgrounds (Binet, 1905, 1908) and thus he continuously cautioned that the test results should be interpreted in light of the school setting and no conclusions concerning acquired or congenital determination of mental abilities should be ascribed to these test results; also Binet cautioned of the need for different tests (or batteries of tests) for persons of differing backgrounds (Binet, 1908; Goodenough, 1949; Edwards, 1971).

INTELLIGENCE ASSESSMENT IN AMERICA

Early American Eugenic Movement and Intelligence

Eugenics is the science of improvement of the human race by better breeding (Davenport, 1972). The science of eugenics had its origins in the theories of Darwin and Mendel and was formulated by Sir Frances Galton. Galton expressed eugenics as the science which deals with all influences that improve the inborn qualities of a race. Even in ancient times there appears to be a concern on the part of man to improve on his own species. Plato from a section in the fifth book of his Republic portrayed Socrates asking Glaucon as to how he would breed better men; "Would he not suggest mate best with best, as he would do with his sheep or horses?" (Rouse, 1956). The eugenicists believed that man is an organism - an animal; and the same laws that held for the improvement of corn and of race horses also held true for man. Unless people accepted this simple truth, and let it influence marriage selection, the eugenics felt that human progress would cease.

Galton, and his many followers, in their program of eugenics set forth a form of social control of human evolution by selection (Dunn, 1967; Pickens, 1968). They were interested in influencing the probability that particular genes would be represented in the offsprings of mankind (congruent with the laws of Mendel). However, this envolved a judgment about which genes are desirable and which are undesirable. Little question was raised about the undesirability of certain genes --- such as those for crippling diseases, idiocies, and severe mental or physical retardation. However, when the undesirable gene deals with that of inborn mental ability much more of a problem arises. Galton felt that such a gene for inborn mental ability existed, and that success itself was the criterion for its evaluation; "social, financial, or intellectual eminence was the proof that the genes were there." (Dunn, 1967).

Charles Davenport, David S. Jordon, Edward M. East and Harry H. Laughlin, drawing heavily from naturalistic philosophy and Sir Frances Galton, constructed a philosophy for the eugenic movement in America (Pickens, 1968). The common denominator in their theories was: (a) that heredity is of supreme importance to man and his civilization; (b) that the unfit must be eliminated or at least limited in number and (c) that the fit must be encouraged to increase in their numbers. These objectives were to be achieved through a scientific knowledge and social application of heredity.

Eugenicists, although Darwinists, distrusted the nebulously unscientific aspect of natural selection (Pickens, 1968). They generally felt that a man of sound heredity could overcome any disadvantage in his socioeconomic environment and win the positions of status and power in the social order. However, Blacks in the United States had not done so --- in fact had not

Galton himself stated that races vary in intelligence, and suggested that negroes are very probably two grades below whites (Pintner, 1931). This opinion already had strong support in the American community, as numerous American history books will show. However, one problem existed --- the inferiors (Blacks) were breeding faster than their superiors (Dunn, 1967; Pickens, 1968; Davenport, 1911) thus eugenicists believed that in the long run the effect would be a swamping of the social order in a sea of stupidity; many admitted though this was only speculation (Holmes, 1933).

Charles B. Davenport (1886-1944) was to the American eugenicists what Sir Francis Galton was to British eugenicists; and in his writings from 1904-1940 Davenport constantly expressed racist-eugenic ideals (Pickens, 1968). Davenport believed that members of other (non-white) races were, in effect, members of different elementary species (Pickens, 1968; Davenport and Steggerda, 1970; Davenport, 1972). Davenport felt that mental, moral, and intellectual aspects of racial development maintained these differences and that man's general reactions, whether violent or repressed, were the product of his hereditary temperament. Thus he wrote, a hyberdized people are a badly put together people and a dissatisfied, restless, ineffective people. Racial intermarriage leads only to disharmony of physical, mental and temperamental qualities and this means also disharmony with environment (Pickens, 1968; Davenport, 1972). Needless to say, Davenport favored segregation. He in fact considered it a scientific social policy, necessary for social stability and order

(Pickens, 1968). Since Davenport was the spokesman for the eugenic movement in America, these same views of Black genetic inferiority and the hereditability of mental abilities characterized the philosophy of the eugenic movement in America.

Out of the eugenic movement came two major solutions to achieving racial improvement - birth control and sterilization of the unfit (Blacks and Whites proven to be genetically inferior).

Although the controversy over Social Darwinism first centered around the religious significance of Darwin's theories, the racial implications gained in importance as the century passed. As the controversy became more racial in content, the debate affected the climate of opinion and Social Darwinism was accepted (the inheritance of acquired characteristics and the survival of the fittest). "This theory explained the innate superiority of Western Europeans at a time when Americans sought personal assurance of their racial purity. America was great because its people were superior, and they were superior because they were Anglo-Saxon." (Pickens, 1968).

By 1930, geneticists had destroyed the eugenic aspiration (Dobzhansky, 1941, 1955, 1964, 1967; Pickens, 1968; Ludmerer, 1972) of wanting to control genetic make-up by selective breeding; saying that in rejecting or selecting an organism Nature is not concerned with the origin of its adaptation. Divested from environmental luck the organism can only transmit its hereditary capabilities. Perfection in a species, therefore, is not possible, but exists only as a statistical character in a given population (Hardin, 1961).

Psychology in America did not escape the impact of eugenics. The concept of recapitulation taught by Thomas Huxley, Charles Darwin's leading disciple (Pickens, 1968) that the development of the brain followed the evolutionary history of the race. Further, Darwinists conceptualized that the embryo --- of any animal, including man, passed through the adult stages of its evolutionary ancestors. These and other concepts of recapitulation became popular with child psychologists. From the belief that behavior if innate, not learned, came the theory of instinct psycgology (Pickens, 1968). Other examples of the effects of the eugenic movement on American psychological thought could be sighted; however, for the sake of expiditation only one additional will be mentioned. One felt to be of utmost significance to an inquiry into the development of mental (intelligence) testing in America.

As stated earlier, some scientists felt that by testing the weak-minded could be discovered and thus brought under society's control (whether for placement into special classes as with Binet, 1905, 1908; or for the eugenic purpose of eliminating misfits). An interest in eugenics and Medelian inheritance encouraged the introduction of Binet's testing methods in the United States (Davies, 1959; Pickens, 1968; Zach, 1972). Henry H. Goddard, director of a New Jersey Institute for the Feebleminded (The Training School at Vineland) in search of a device to differentiate between children regarded as of normal or subnormal mentalities came across Binet's report of his 1908 scale and being impressed with the Binet scale translated it into English with only such minor changes as were necessary to make it applicable for use with American children (Goodenough, 1949). After satisfying himself of its usefulness by trying it on a few cases (400 inmates of Vineland Institute) Goddard published his scale in 1910. As a check he further administered the test to 2000 children in the Vineland Public Schools with the results demonstrating that the test differentiated between normal and feebleminded children (Goddard, 1911). "The intellectual backwardness of these children was manifested not only in their low test scores but by their inability to do work of their school grades," Goddard concluded (Goodenough, 1949). Thus the assumption appears to be that normal from Goddard's research is equated with the ability to do school related work - which is in essence what Binet had professed the test to differentiate --- between those students who would do well in the schools (of Paris) and those who would not (Binet 1905-1908). However, Goddard's later classification gave a mental-age valuation to such words as idiots, imbeciles, and morons based on the importance of heredity (Davies, 1959; Pickens, 1968). Upon what data could Goddard have reached such a conclusion? Definitely not the research he had done, and Binet had insisted that no such conclusions could be drawn from his work. "As long as any given strain is kept pure, we will have, the same mental capacity and possibilities generation after generation," but inbreeding and crossbreeding produce new combinations which will not be pure (Goddard, 1912). Pickens (1968) has said that "the sum of Goddard's

43

efforts suggested hereditary determinism in regard to mental ability." The belief that Goddard theorized --- a hereditary determination of mental abilities seems to be supported by his many books (Goddard, 1911, 1912, 1914) and further confirmed in the writings of Pickens (1968) and Zach (1972).

It is unfortunate that this person who introduced mental testing measurements into the United States is so directly linked to the eugenic movement in America. Especially since Goddard used the results of his test to substantiate the theories of the movement: (a) that some races are genetically inferior to others and thus mixing the races would lead to a dilution of the genetic pool, and (b) that mental abilities were heritable. It appears that Goddard personally, and many of those who followed him, took only a slightly modified translation of Binet's original scale and assigned to it the ability to differentiate between the innate inheritable qualities of individuals (in essence the ability to differentiate between genetically superior and inferior peoples and races). Goddard, the eugenicists, and many other researchers and scientists reached such conclusions from test results which the authors (Binet and Simon, 1905, 1908) and others (Stern, 1914) so repeatedly cautioned: (a) were simply a reflection of differences between the abilities of individuals to perform or not to perform in a school setting; (b) that attempts to define the results of the test as acquired or congenital or even to ascertain the etiology of one's functioning was beyond the realm of the measurement and (c) that the test results reflected higher scores on the average of one and one-half years for persons of superior social classes, when compared with the poor child for whom it was designed (Binet, 1908; Decrolyn and Degand, 1910). Are we thus to conclude that simply by translating the Binet Scale of 1908 into English and making only slight modifications to accommodate American children, Goddard converted the scale from one which was designed to assess educability of school children (Edwards, 1971) and to be used in a school setting (Goodenough, 1949) to one which reflected heritable mental abilities and supported the theory of the genetic superiority of one race (Caucasiod) over another (Negroid in particular and others in general)?

Few people question that mental deficiency tends to run in families. Especially when the deficiency is so severe as to be characterized as idiotic (as defined by Binet in 1908). However, Goddard in his books The Kallikak Family, (1912) and Feeblemindedness; Its Causes and Consequences, (1914) stressed mental deficiency as the "soil from which such social ills as delinquency and crime, sexual promiscuity with its accompanying evils of venereal disease and illegitimacy, drunkenness, and pauperism, commonly spring." This coupled with Goddard's stress of the heritability of all mental abilities and his eugenic views on the genetic inferiority of the Black race in America lead to the conclusion that by using his test society could detect and thus control many of the serious social ills through selective breeding and sterilization of misfits.

Goddard's research with delinquents and criminals tended to support his assumptions that the social misfits of society were feebleminded --- in that on the average, populations of such groups scores three or more years below average on his revised Binet scale. Such discoveries were reassuring to eugenicists (and psychologists as well) since at least they had found a measure which would differentiate, at an early age, between those mental defectives (Pickens, 1968).

As more data, however, on test results became available; especially those which showed a marked tendency toward a downward shift in test standing with advancing age - a fact which suggested that the standards at the older levels were too difficult (Goodenough, 1949; and as earlier reported by Decrolyn and Degand, 1910) and the findings which showed such marked differences between test and retest scores; questions as to the infallibility of the tests became more frequent.

That the evidence upon which the data obtained by Goddard were based was flimsy few people at the time appeared to notice - whether this was due to a lack of knowledge or an apathy on the part of eugenicists and those who held similar views is not known. However, since neither the era of scientific criticism of tests and of testing standards, nor that of advanced insights and study of the laws of inheritance according to the laws of Mendel has arrived then there should be little doubt as to the sincere attempts on the part of Goddard and his assistants to scientifically (within the limits of the time) ascertain such a valid measure to in fact differentiate between mental defective and normal children (Goodenough, 1949).

Even during the early life of the tests of mental abilities, many criticisms were made, stating that the tests were too linguistic in character; and thus children from foreign homes or those with only a limited knowledge of English were unjustly handicapped. Goddard's crusading zeal and his unchallenged acceptance of Darwinistic principles of natural selection and Mendelian laws of inheritance often appeared to blind him to sources of error in his work and to possible erroneous conclusions which in light of modern science seems glaringly apparent (Goodenough, 1949).

Later Intelligence Testing in America

Like Binet, who had challenged the sensory-motor approach as a method of measuring higher mental abilities, Lewis M. Terman challenged the sensory motor approach and became a highly vocal advocate of the Binet method in America. In 1906 Terman published an article, "Genius and Stupidity" (Terman, 1906) in which he directed attention to the Binet approach, and which served as the stimulus which gave a new impetus to the mental-testing movement in America.

In Terman's earlier studies to ascertain a suitable measure of the mental capabilities of the individual he based his research on the Binet experimental studies of intelligence of 1902 (Terman, 1906; Edwards, 1971). Terman in an attempt to identify different extremes in intellectual competence went to teachers in the school system of Worcester, Massachusetts and asked them to estimate among the boys enrolled in their classes those who were the brightest and the dullest. Twenty-four boys were identified, with half of them believed to be exceptionally bright and the other half exceptionally dull. Of the twenty-four selected, fourteen participated in the study. The study continued six hours a day, six days per week from January through May 1905. Terman concluded from data received as a result of giving Binet test, and from other sources, that bright boys were superior to dull boys in all of the mental tasks (inventiveness and creative imagination; logical processes; mathematical ability; language mastery; insight; ease of acquisition; and power of memory), but inferior to them in the set of motor tasks (Terman, 1906; Edwards, 1971). One can see that Terman, like Binet, directed his attention toward the school setting, advocating that there should be attempts to determine the qualitative nature of retardation and acceleration, both in terms of the native intellectual endowment of the child and in terms of educational outcomes (Edwards, 1971).

Terman, like Goddard and the eugenics saw intelligence as having a possible genetic heritability (Bayley, 1970). Thus in the 1916 Stanford Revision of Binet's test, Terman popularizing the concept of IQ, followed Galtonian tradition in the study of individual differences and assumed that race was the basis for these differences (Pickens, 1968).

The Stanford 1916 revision of the Binet-Simon tests was said to be the first real revision of the scale in America; the others had simply been translations (Goodenough, 1949). This revision introduced many new items and changed the location, method of administering, or the scoring of others. The intelligence quotient as the basic way of expressing test results, introduced by Stern in 1914, was accepted and made popular by Terman in the 1916 revision.

A series of clear and well-organized instructions for administering and scoring the tests was provided. Fractional scores were avoided by providing six items at each yearly age level.

It appears that basically Terman was interested in the standardization of the Binet scale - and interest which had occupied his time for the five to six years previous to his 1916 revision (Goodenough, 1949). Most of the item changes in this revision were the result of empirical studies of the original Binet scale which had proven the item to be of little diagnostic value. Terman's manual, giving precise instructions for administering, scoring and the effects of deviations from the standard procedure, further popularized the use and acceptance of his revision.

After reviewing the literature and examining both the Binet Scales and the 1916 Stanford revision it appears that Terman's revision was simply a more empirical way of administering and scoring a basically similar Binet Scale with a new method of expressing the test results (IQ) added. Nothing that could (or should) have lead one to believe that a new test had been devised was therein --- one which could now differentiate between the acquired and congenital nature of higher mental abilities - or intelligence.

Terman, however, should not be credited with professing that intelligence was the sole result of genetic inheritance; although it can be shown that he believed that genetics (or innate capacities) account for the greater proportion of these higher mental capacities (Terman, 1906, 1912; Goodenough, 1949; Pickens, 1968; Edwards, 1971). Terman on many occasions cautioned and attested to problems concerning differences in scores made as a result of differences in cultural levels of the home from which the child comes (Pickens, 1968). However, many persons (psychologists and otherwise) dazzled by the numerous reports of the marked contrasts in school achievement and general behavior of children with high and low IQ's, the Darwinist-Galtonist theories and the eugenic philosophy "became all too ready to accept the test results as a final criterion by which a child's potential abilities might be determined once and for all" (Goodenough, 1949).

For twenty-one years the Stanford 1916 revision of the Binet Scale maintained the leading position among the intelligence tests used in both the United States and abroad; "so great was the confidence in this scale that many people came to identify a Stanford-Binet IQ with intelligence itself" (Goodenough, 1949). However, because of imperfections in the scale, especially those dealing with problems which arose as a result of less than perfect standardization procedures for the extreme ranges (test too easy for younger children and too difficult for older ones - Decrolyn and Degand, 1910; Binet, 1908) and those dealing with the need for an alternate form when a retest was called for, lead to the 1937 Stanford Revision.

Other criticisms and possible revisions on the Binet Scales were suggested. However, most were simply translations of the original scales. Robert M. Yerkes and associates proposed a revision in a paper dated 1915 (Yerkes, Bridges and Hardwick, 1915). This proved to be what has been characterized as an alternative method in scoring. Yerkes suggested a table of standards showing

50

the average number of test items passed by children at successive chronological ages as an alternative to the point method of scoring used by Binet. He believed that such a system would enhance the discriminative value of the original Binet Scale.

Other tests of intelligence in America were being developed during the early years of the twentieth century. After the declaration of war with Germany in 1917, psychologists of the American Psychological Association lead by Yerkes took data not yet published by Arthur S. Otis, based on earlier objective tests by Courtis, 1908, and developed the first group test of intelligence - the Army Alpha. Later the Army Beta test constructed to be used with illiterates was developed. These early group tests were used to differentiate between those draftees who were possibly unfit for military services as well as those who might be suitable as officer training candidates. After the war, many psychologists who had been employed in these testing programs as well as others impressed with the simplicity of administration --- and the reports of the effectiveness with which the test had been employed in the Army, set to work constructing other group tests after the same general model to be used in educational settings (Goodenough, 1949). Many of the now revised group tests of intelligence were developed during this period. A complete listing of such tests would not serve any real purpose here - but such tests as the Otis Primary Examination; The National Intelligence Test (Haggerty, Terman, Thorndike, Whipple and Yerkes); The Otis Group Intelligence Scale; Thurstone Psychological Examination; and Thorndike Intelligence Examination, were among these early tests.

Such tests included non-language tests; non-verbal tests and verbal tests (See Pintner, 1931 for a more complete listing). Goodenough (1949) has especially noted the blind faith which many people displayed in the results obtained from such tests. Stating that although statistical methods as a means of demonstrating the worth of such devices were coming into full swing, only a few of the test makers had more than a rudimentary understanding of the procedure about which they talked so glibly. Although discussions of the reliability and validity of such tests dominated the programs of psychological meetings and conferences "many of the participants failed to realize that if two measures are correlated at all, a coefficient of almost any desired magnitude can be obtained by making the range of talent over which it is computed sufficiently long" (Goodenough, 1949). Thus IQ's obtained from half a dozen different group tests were "joyfully computed and entered on children's permanent record cards by teachers and principals with as much assurance as their grandfathers had placed in the skull maps drawn up by their favorite phrenologists" (Goodenough, 1949).

With the introduction and widespread use of statistical techniques in the study of psychology many correlations were made between intelligence, as measured by mental tests, and other variables --- especially many variables that were known to be biologically (or genetically) determined (Herskovits, 1926; Klineberg, 1928; Goodenough, 1949; Pintner, 1931; Edwards, 1971). When intelligence as defined by the various measurement devices was found to be highly positively correlated with many of these biological factors, it was concluded that the probability of intelligence also

52

being inherited (or genetically determined) was significantly
high enough to be accepted. Jensen (1969) stated that since intelligence is basically dependent on the structural and bio-
chemical properties of the brain, it should not be surprising
that differences in intellectual capacity are partly the result
of genetic factors which conform to the same principles involved
in the inheritance of physical characteristics. The general model
for the facts of inheritance of continuous or metrical physical
traits, such as stature and fingerprint ridges, also applies to
intelligence; stated Jensen. The mechanism of inheritance for
such traits is called polygenic, since normal variation in the
characteristic is the result of multiple genes whose effects are
small, similar, and cumulative. However, what such correlational
procedures failed to note (or at least to mention) is that as
stated by Goodenough (1949), "if two measures are correlated at
all, a coefficient of almost any desired magnitude can be obtained
by making the range of talent over which it is computed sufficiently long."

If statistical techniques are used it can be easily shown
that intelligence is also highly positively correlated with other
biologically determined variables (like width of nose, color of
eyes, and the texture of hair, to name only a few - especially
here in the United States - Herskovits, 1928; Klineberg, 1928).
However, theorists have ceased to assume that knowing, for example,
one's hair color was a good indicator of one's mental abilities
(especially when the subjects concerned are of the same race).
Binet and others, especially those operating from an anthropo-

53

logical frame of reference, had earlier made just such types of assumptions: that the head size of an individual was an indicator of his mental capacities.   However, Binet had abandoned such theories before he made his scale of 1905 (Goodenough, 1949); also such notions have been abandoned by the average psychologist, anthropologist, (Bayley, 1970), and geneticists have informed us that no factor (or factors) have been isolated (as of yet) in the genes as the determiner of intellectual capacity (Dobzhansky, 1941), 1955, 1964, 1967).   Thus the conclusion that mental capacities are transmitted by isolated genes may be simply wishful thinking; perpetuating a self-fulfilling prophesy.

The fallacy today appears to be in the logic of taking correlations that have been found to be statistically correlated with intelligence as measured, and concluding that since these variables are biologically (or genetically) determined, then intelligence also is biologically (or genetically) determined. Since conclusions gleaned from statistical techniques seem to have in fact been formulated and accepted by many psychologists, sociologists, anthropologists, educators, and especially the American public as a truism; then the point that one should be constantly reminded of is that these conclusions: that intelligence is biologically (or genetically) determined - drawn from statistical correlations are only assumptions based on a particular theoretical model.

At present, no empirical data exist to show without a doubt that intelligence is either biologically (genetically) determined or that it is environmentally determined.   However, by reviewing the research either of the two positions can be supported simply by selecting data which is supportive of the position you wish to take (Biehler, 1971; Menacker and Pollack, 1974). The overriding assumption held by most present psychologists appears to be that although genetics may determine the limits of one's mental capacities; the environment sets the level at which one functions (Bayley, 1970); and it is concluded that very few individuals function at their limits.

TYPES OF INTELLIGENCE TESTS AND THEIR THEORETICAL NATURE

As early as 1949 Goodenough stated that differences in the nature of the tests affect their practical use and significance, and suggested that by showing such some of the prevalent misconceptions that have been our heritage from the past --- when practical necessity too often led to the construction of devices that served an immediate purpose but lacked a firm basis in fundamental theory, may be cleared up and the way to future progress indicated (Goodenough, 1949).

That one's stated definitions and theories of intelligence have stimulated the thinking and research efforts of individual psychologists and have led to the development of a host of useful tests of intelligence is not questioned (Reese and Lipsitt, 1970; Bayley, 1970). However, few psychologists have given operational definitions to the concept of intelligence testing, so that such tests can be used interchangeably to measure the same behavioral universe as done in the physical sciences (Spiker and McCandless, 1954).

Intelligence theory has developed from several different prospectives, among them: (a) whether intelligence is a general unitary function consisting of many traits, or a specific function

(Bayley, 1970); and (b) whether intelligence is reflected through sensorimotor tasks or through general factors which comprise higher mental processes (Edwards, 1971).

The general theories of intelligence profess that there are different kinds of higher and more complex mental processes such as reasoning, imagination, etc., that constitute a general unitary function (later called intelligence) and that certain tests (and test items) could be devised to measure these complex processes (Binet, 1908). That all of these higher mental processes are not known does not limit the extent to which one is able to measure the trait. Simply by taking a representative sampling of those known higher mental processes one can get a measure of the intellectual capacity of the individual in question. By the use of mental age, IQ, and appropriate standardization procedures one can make comparisons between individuals; as well as give diagnosis for remediation in the classroom. This theory was given impetus in the works of Binet 1895-1911, and further in the intelligence testing movements throughout the world which followed Binet's lead and theory.

The specific theories of intelligence profess that intelligence is a composite of several more or less independent abilities, and in order to get an adequate estimate of one's intelligence one must test each specific function and calculate this composite (Reese and Lipsitt, 1970). Its impact on the intelligence movement has been tremendous in recent years with J. P. Guilford's Structure of Intellect (SI) theory of human intellect being the most prominent and provocative. Guilford conceived the idea that human intellectual activities could be described in terms of the subdivisions of three major dimensions - operations, products, and contents. Guilford postulates some one hundred twenty separate factors of intelligence with eighty of these factors already known, and is presently researching to ascertain the other forty factors. Guilford's model expand the definition of intelligence beyond the limits of traditional tests and thus has become of major significance in the United States intelligence movement of today (Sarason and Gladwin, 1958; Reese and Lipsitt, 1970).

Early researchers interested in predicting mental abilities (intelligence) worked on the assumption that sensorimotor responses were adequate indicators of these mental abilities (Galton, 1894, 1907, 1914). These assumptions were based on Galtonian theories and given impetus by early German psychologists such as Wundt (Edwards, 1971). Later, with the works of Binet (1895-1908), in France and Terman (1906-1916) in America, a movement away from this sensorimotor approach to the measurement of higher mental processes and toward a sampling approach was begun. Binet suggested that the assumption: discrimination of sensorimotor data reflects intellectual differences (as Galton had accepted) was a false assumption (Edwards, 1971). Binet instead suggested that an individual may be slow in reaction time relative to discrete sensory stimulation, yet not be slow in other forms of behavior (Binet and Henri, 1896). Binet, included sensorimotor tasks in his measure, however, suggesting that it was but a limited part of the overall higher mental processes.

It appears that the majority of the measurement devices (tests) of intelligence (especially those used in American educational settings) have evolved from Binet's theoretical model, and are divided according to the manner of their administration into individual and group tests. The first such tests were individual --- given to each child separately by an examiner who asked questions and then recorded the child's responses, or supervised his drawings and written responses. This procedure insures the subjects greatest attention to and effort in appropriately carrying out the tasks at hand and enhances the validity and reliability of the scores (Bayley, 1970). However, because individual testing is a very time-consuming and expensive procedure, group tests were developed. Group tests were adapted to obtain scores on large numbers of persons in a short period of time; using printed forms and pencils. Group tests are widely used in schools, in military installations and other situations where it is important to test large numbers quickly. Group tests work best with testees who can read, who are familiar with the pencil and paper operations required, and who are well motivated to succeed (Bayley, 1970). Group tests, however, sacrifice some of its reliability for the sake of speed.

An extensive listing and evaluation of the theoretical nature of tests of intelligence presently in existence is beyond the scope of this paper. (For a complete listing see Buros' Mental Measurements Yearbooks, 1938, 1940, 1946, 1953, 1959, 1965, 1972). However, a representative sampling of those tests presently used in educational settings will be evaluated and their theoretical nature pointed out to show how the theoretical basis of tests may determine to a great extent what is reflected by the measurement instrument (test).

Individual Tests

The early tests of mental abilities already mentioned were individual tests - the Binet Scales, Goddard's Translation, Terman's 1916 Revision. A discussion into their theoretical nature and thus what they reflect has been given previously, therefore, this section will deal with tests other than those already mentioned.

In 1937 Terman and Merril published an extensively revised Stanford-Binet Scale with equivalent forms, L and M, to be used when a retest of a subject was necessary and to account for errors which had been found in the 1916 Scale. Whereas, the 1916 Stanford Revision covered the ages two years to superior adult - later research, however, showed that the standardization was less adequate for the two-and three-year tests (Bayley, 1970). Another revision, in 1960, updated some of the materials, and offered a single form, L-M, which was a selection of the best parts of Scales L and M and with improved norms for years two and three (Bayley, 1970). In the 1960 Stanford revision, the CA/MA ratio for finding IQ was dropped, and instead deviation IQs were derived from the means and standard deviations of the mental age scores obtained by the standardization sample. There were little changes in the theoretical nature of either the 1937 or the 1960 Stanford Revisions, and Terman still viewed intelligence as being genetically determined (Bayley, 1970).

Because the original Benit Scales, and the Stanford Revision of 1916 (Freeman, 1955), were not suited for use with adults (Decrolyn and Degand, 1906, 1910; Binet and Simon, 1908) and even though the Stanford-Binet Scale of 1937 was better standardized and included three superior adult levels - with many researchers questioning their adequacy for adults (Freeman, 1955) there was a need for a more adequate means of measuring adult intelligence.

Intelligence testing of adults was begun on a large scale in 1917 with the introduction of the Army Alpha (verbal) and Army Beta (non-verbal) tests. Although this movement provided the impetus for the development of a number of group tests for adults, these tests and the ones to follow proved to be adequate for only a select group of the adult population (Freeman, 1955).

Thus in 1939 the Weschler-Bellevue Scale of Intelligence was introduced, supposedly as an effective scale for the measurement of adolescent and adult intelligence. The Bellevue Scale was intended to test a combination of verbal and non-verbal materials from the ages of ten through sixty years, with norms beginning at age seven and a half years.

The theory behind the construction of the Bellevue test was based on the principle that intelligence involves not only ability to deal with symbols, abstractions, and conceptual thinking, but that it also involves ability to deal with situations and problems in which concrete objects, rather than words and numbers, are utilized. Wechsler thus adapted a general-factor theory of intelligence, which required that the scale in its totality should provide a valid index of the individual's general ability. Wechsler further decided that both verbal and non-verbal materials would provide the most adequate and representative content for the scale --- rather than either one alone. Thus he proceeded to select the particular types of subtest which had been widely used and valided by other psychologists (Freeman, 1955). Therefore, the types of items included in Wechsler's Scale were not unique. They were selected from available sources after a study had been made of a variety of standardized tests then in use, including the Binet and Stanford-Binet Scales (Freeman, 1955). The Wechsler-Bellevue Scale consisted of eleven parts, or subtests; six being verbal: (1) Information, (2) General Comprehension, (3) Arithmetical Reasoning, (4) Memory span for digits, forward and backward, (5) Similarities and (6) Vocabulary; and five non-verbal: (1) Picture arrangement, (2) Picture completion, (3) Block design, (4) Object assembly and (5) Digit-symbol test. The Scale thus enabled three scores to be obtained: (1) Full Scale Score, (2) Verbal Score and (3) Performance score; with the possibility of computing an individual IQ score for each scale score.

For the sample population Wechsler used 1081 literate individuals (all White) divided into ten comprehensive occupational categories (based upon occupational distributions of the country's adults as shown by the 1930 United States Census), with ages ranging from seventeen to seventy. This adult population's educational status was compared with that of the U.S. population at large - with the assumption being that a similar distribution

of educational levels of the standardized group would provide
further evidence of its representative character (Freeman, 1955).
(However, it was found that the educational level of the standardization group was higher than that of the general population, although the range of both groups was from college graduate to
illiterate.) Because the Bellevue Scale was standardized for some
ages below the adult level a younger age population was also needed.
The chosen criterion was the age-grade distribution of pupils in
the public schools of New York City (1300 children); and selected
representative and average schools in the New York and New Jersey
areas (200 children), ranging in ages from seven to sixteen years.
From these 1500 students 670 subjects (all White) were selected to
yield an age-grade distribution that would fairly well approximate
that of the New York City school population.

The Scale was validated in several ways: (1) Intercorrelations of Subtests - which were necessary to provide data with regard to the presence or absence of a "g-factor" (See Wechsler, 1944
for complete correlations). (2) Correlation with Schooling - as
recalled the amount of schooling or quality of educational achievement (or both) were used as criteria for validity by Binet (Goodenough, 1949; Freeman, 1955) and later by both Goddard and Terman
(and for almost all other intelligence tests). So too was the
Bellevue Scale validated; with scores on the Bellevue correlated
to the number of years in school being .64. (3) Correlation with
Teacher's Judgments - teacher's estimates of pupils intelligence
rated on a six-point scale was used with correlations for a group
of adolescents (74 in number) in a trade school being .52; and

for another group (45 in number) in the general high school being
.43. (4) Increase and decrease of scores with increasing age -
showing rises of mean scores until age twenty-two and a half years,
then slowly declining (which is inconsistent with norms of other
tests - Freeman, 1955). (5) Constancy of means and Standard Deviation of IQs at various ages - accepted as reasonably constant and
as a good satisfaction of this criterion (Freeman, 1955). (6)
Range and Distribution of intelligence quotients - from about 45 to
145 for a population of 1508 cases (ages ten to sixty years). A
negatively skewed distribution with a slightly narrower range above
100 than below. Wechsler did not believe the assumption that a
symmetrical, ball-shaped distribution (Gausian) was necessary as
Terman had believed and as Binet had implied (Freeman, 1955).
(7) Known groups - taking groups known to be of specific intelligence (in this case a borderline group with IQs of sixty-six and
seventy-nine and a mentally defective group with IQs of fifty and
sixty-five) and correlating their scores on each subtest. The main
scores on each subtest did differentiate and was in the expected
direction (Wechsler, et al, 1941). (8) Correlation with the
Stanford-Binet - a common practice is correlating one test of intelligence with another. Correlation yielded a coefficient of .82;
and what is considered most significant (9) Wechsler's statement
as to how he know his test was a good measure of intelligence.
"The only honest reply we can make is that our experience has shown
them to be so. If this seems to be a tenuous answer we need only
remind the reader that it has been practical experience which has
given (or denied) final validity to every other intelligence

64

test ... Empirical judgments, here as elsewhere, play the role of utlimate arbiter. In any case, all evidence for the validity of a test, whether statistical or otherwise, is inevitably of an indirect sort and, in the end, cumulative rather than decisive," Wechsler, 1946).

As for reliability of the Bellevue scale, Freeman (1955) stated that very little research was done in its early years even though the Bellevue was in widespread use especially in clinical areas. Wechsler's manual itself reports only very meager and in-adequate data on reliability; namely, 52 individuals retested at intervals of one month to one year (Freeman, 1955). Further, Freeman states that it appears that only one investigation using a fairly adequate sampling of individuals to ascertain the reli-ability of the Bellevue scale for use with normal subjects was done by 1950; that one being done by Derner, Aborn and Canter in the Journal of Consulting Psychology, 1950.

From the above review it appears that the Wechsler-Bellevue Scale was an extention of the Binet and Stanford-Revision of the Binet Scales, with the introduction of a performance score (de-rived from the group testing movement), and a full scale score that was a combination of verbal and non-verbal (performance) materials. A principal difference occurring in item arrangement between the Bellevue Scale and those of the Binet and Stanford-Binet Scales - with the Bellevue Scale having all items of one type grouped to-gether thus constituting a subtest of the whole; and the Binet and Stanford-Binet Scales having items of various types grouped together at each age level, thus testing a variety of functions.

There appears to be no indication here of a test being devised which was capable of getting at some innate inheritable trait, and the point is often made that like all tests of information and vocabulary, performance on these in the Bellevue is dependent, in part, upon opportunity to learn, whether in school, home or through the intellectual exploitation of all aspects of one's environment (Freeman, 1955). It appears to be the implicit assumption that by introducing performance items which place very little premium upon educational or other cultural advantages the Bellevue Scale score will be less affected by cultural differences.

The 1955 revision of the Bellevue Scale (known as the Wechsler Adult Intelligence Scale) although meeting some of the adverse criticisms of the earlier scale did not introduce any new principles in its content, construction, organization, scoring, or IQ derivation. The main changes were in the revision of some content, extension of the population sample, and improvement in directions for administering and scoring (Freeman, 1955). Other Wechsler scales were devised using the same basic theoretical nature as that of the original Bellevue Scale. They include the Wechsler Intelligence Scale for Children (WISC-1949); for children five through fifteen years of age, and the Wechsler Preschool and Primary Scale of Intelligence (WPPSI-1949-1967); for children ages four to six and a half.

Other individual tests of a performance (non-verbal) nature were devised. These are tests in which the use of language is eliminated from test content and responses, although directions are generally given orally a few instances exist where directions too, are given without the use of language by using pantomime techniques. Performance (non-verbal) tests were first devised as a supplement to, and substitute for, the Stanford-Binet Scale in order to examine deaf, illiterate, or non-English speaking subjects (Freeman, 1955). Since their introduction, however, the use of the non-verbal tests has been extended to be utilized with children who have or are suspected of having reading difficulties; with persons who may have been handicapped by markedly inferior environmental conditions, or by examiners who believe, for any reason, that such a scale will yield a more complete picture of the individual whose capacities are being analyzed and evaluated.

Such performance scales include the Pintner-Paterson Scale of Performance Tests (1917), the first to be organized into a scale, and one which has been incorporated into many of the newer scales including the Wechsler (Freeman, 1955).

Individual scales have been devised to evaluate mental development of subjects ranging in age from one month to six years. These scales, for the most part, are not tests in the usual sense, but rather, are norms and inventories of development and behavior grouped at their respective average age levels, and derived from observations of children's behavior and from experimentation in a variety of situations (Freeman, 1955). These type schedules include the works of: Gesell with infants and young children at Yale Clinic of Development (Gesell, 1925; Gesell and Amatruda, 1947; Gesell and Thompson, 1938) and Piaget with his study of Swiss children (Piaget and Inhelder, 1958, 1973; Piaget, 1951, 1962, 1969a, 1969b, 1970, 1971).

Cattell devised what has been called a developmental and intelligence scale which covers ages two to thirty months; with its items being adaptations of many earlier tests, including those of Gesell and his associates. Cattell states that his scale "...has been so constructed as to constitute an extension downward of Form L of the Stanford-Binet tests .... Thus, using the infant test items for the early months and the Stanford-Binet tests for the older ages with a mixture of the two between, one continuous scale from early infancy to maturity has been attained." (Cattell, 1940). Cattell's method of scoring is the same as that used with the Stanford-Binet scale --- each item is scored as plus or minus with no partial credits given.

With many of the infant developmental scales, no traditional test of validity is given because the builders have no criteria of maturity levels to use as a basis of comparison (Freeman, 1955). They do, however, present a rationale of their schedules as a basis for its validity. Fundamentally the validity of his scale depend on the validity of the norms, the legitimacy of the category classifications, the appropriateness of each item for the category to which it was allocated, the soundness of the concept of maturity level, and the justness of using a sample of the child's behavior to indicate that level; said Gesell (Gesell and Thompson, 1938). Further Gesell stated that his conclusions regarding the validity of his scales go beyond experimental data and are based on years of clinical experience. However, with Cattell's Developmental and Intelligence Scale, although percent passing each item at successive ages was used as evidence of validity, the principal criterion was the correlation between Cattell scale IQ ratings and Stanford-Binet (1937) IQs obtained with the same children. Thus making Cattell's Scale an extension downward of the Stanford-Binet Scale, having a similar theoretical nature and presumed to measure the same mental abilities which were in essence, a reflection of school related abilities (Good-enough, 1949; Cattell, 1940; Edwards, 1971); and which also was what the Binet Scales supposedly measured (Edwards, 1971; Zach, 1972).

Group Tests

Group tests, mentioned previously, were devised in 1917 by a team of army psychologists to ascertain reasonably accurately and rapidly the intellectual levels of vast numbers of men to be inducated for service during World War I. Thus the Army Alpha Scale (verbal) and the Army Beta Scale (non-verbal) were organized and used as group tests. These tests were the product of several psychologists, notably Arthur S. Otis (Freeman, 1955). These group tests, with few exceptions, are constructed on the principle that intelligence is a general capacity and that it should be measured by means of sampling a variety of mental activities (Freeman, 1955). (It should be recalled that this is also the basic theoretical nature of Binet's Scale - Binet, 1908; Good-enough, 1949; Edwards, 1971). Test items (on most of the various scales) include in various combinations such items as: following directions, arithmetical problems, practical judgment (in connec-tion with common-sense problems), word meaning, disarranged sentences, completion of number series, completion of sentences,

verbal analogies, information, mazes, three-dimensional visual-
ization and counting of cubes, symbol-digit combinations, picture
absurdities, picture arrangement, geometrical construction (paper-
form-board), and geometric pattern analogies. Thus test materials
on these various group tests were not all innovations, and had in
fact been used during the early testing movement of the late
nineteenth century in both the United States and several European
countries (Freeman, 1955). On most group scales, items of each
type are placed together in separate subtests or parts, beginning
with the easiest and progressing by intervals (as equal as possible) to the most difficult. It is assumed that by arranging the
items thusly, every individual for whom the test is intended
should be able to get some items correct and to proceed to a level
of difficulty which represents his maximum in that particular type
of mental activity (Freeman, 1955).

Generally, the various group scales are scored by taking
an individual's score in terms of the number of points earned (raw
score), looking for that raw score in a table of norms and con-
verting to a mental age, from which an intelligence quotient (IQ)
is calculated. Manuals usually accompany most group tests giving
various tables of norms and sometimes percentile ranks by age or
grade. Most group tests impose time limits for each of the several
subtests with some scales being entirely non-verbal in content
(Pintner-Cunningham Primary Test (1938) form A and B for children
in kindergarten, grade one and the first half of grade two; Army
Beta Examination (1917) for illiterates and non-English speaking
men in the Army of World War I; the Revised Army Beta Examination

(1935) a test for relatively illiterate or non-English speakers, but for the general population; Progressive Matrices Tests (1938) to evaluate subjects ability to apprehend relationships between geometric figures and designs - or ability to discern and utilize a logical relationship presented by non-verbal materials; Cattell's Culture-Free Test (1944) to measure general mental ability free from verbal materials and free from acquired skills measured by most performance tests (Cattell, 1944); and Goodenough's Drawing Test (1926) to evaluate a child's intelligence by means of his drawing of a man. For a complete listing and explanation of the various non-verbal group tests see Buros Mental Measurement Yearbooks, 1938, 1940, 1946, 1953, 1959, 1965 and 1972). Other group tests are entirely verbal; or a combination of the two types of items (California Test of Mental Maturity (1951) on five levels: preprimary (kindergarten and entering grade 1); primary (grade 1-3); elementary (grades 4-8); intermediate (grades 7-10 and adult); and advanced (grade 9 and adult). Chicago Tests of Primary Mental Abilities (Thurstone and Thurstone, 1938) for ages 11-17 based upon the theory that intelligence consists of the operations of certain distinguishable and relatively independent mental functions (group-factor theory); The Kuhlmann-Anderson Tests (1927) with many revisions (1927-1952), includes nine scales graded according to school level and includes thirty-nine subtests from kindergarten (subtest 1-10) through grades 9-12 (subtests 30-39); and the Otis Group Intelligence Scale (1919) in two examinations ranging from kindergarten through 12th grade; Otis also devised tests designed to be self-administering and/or quick scoring. For a more detailed listing and explanation see (Buros

71

Mental Measurement Yearbooks, 1938, 1940, 1946, 1953, 1959, 1965, 1972).

The majority of group tests, both verbal and non-verbal, have been validated by using all, or a combination of one or more, of the following: test performance of retarded, average, and accelerated pupils; intercorrelations of subtests; correlations of subtests with total scores; means, standard deviations, and ranges of IQs at the several grade levels; correlations with quality of school work; power to discriminate among successive age groups; and correlations with various other intelligence tests (especially the Stanford-Binet Scale of 1916-Freeman, 1955).

Thus most group scales are based, implicitly at least, upon the general factor theory of intelligence (Freeman, 1955). Most group tests undertake to sample a person's mental activities by means of several kinds of tasks and then to rate the individual by means of a single index. However, a few scales are based upon the group-factor theory.

On the basis of data reported in a hugh volume detailing the psychological use of group testing in the Army during World War I (Yerkes, 1921) many periodical articles and books appeared on such subjects as racial and national differences in intelligence, geographic differences in intelligence within the United States, differences between occupational groups, relationship between educational status and intelligence, and the general intellectual level of the American adult. "Not only were many of these data of doubtful validity but some of the interpretations

and publications based upon them gave rise to serious misapprehensions in regard to the foregoing problems, which are loaded with
social and educational implications." (Freeman, 1955).

MEASURED IQ SCORES - WHAT THEY REFLECT

At the international symposium of 1921 held in Boston to express views on the nature of intelligence, E. G. Boring created a mild sensation by proposing the use of a purely operational definition for intelligence - that intelligence is <u>what the tests test</u> (Goodenough, 1949). Boring said that frequently we have little more than a name, which is variously understood by different people, and as such only the test maker can inform us about the nature of the behavioral universe of which the test is presumed to be a sample. Often when test makers have taken care to define their terms - but when everyday terms such as intelligence, egocentricity, dominance, etc., are used, people who later use the method, too often will interpret the results of the test according to their own preconceived notions of the meaning of the term, which may or may not agree with those of the person devising the test (Goodenough, 1949). Such appears to have happened with the results gleaned from the Binet Scale. Many psychologists (Goddard, Terman, Jensen, etc.) took the test results and because of their basic personal theoretical backgrounds, interpreted these results in a manner that was obviously not intended by Binet (Binet, 1908; Binet and Simon, 1973).

Boring's suggestion implied that the tests should be re-
garded as <u>a sign</u> and not as <u>a sample</u> of the trait being measured.
Goodenough (1949) further suggested that a sign method would be
more appropriate than the sample method in use at this time (and
which comprises the majority of present methods) because a trait
seems to imply something inherent in the individual, and has a
greater chance of being thought that the measure is an accurate
predictor of the behavior; when in fact such is not the case.
Further caution has been given as to Trait Name. Goodenough
again stated that two authors, even though testing the same trait
may have completely different ideas as to the universes to which
the same name applies and thus the sample tasks which they include
in their tests may have little or nothing in common to each other.

A look at what authors of various mental abilities (intelligence) tests, themselves, say their tests reflect may give
us more insight and possibly highlight when and where tests ceased
to reflect a sampling of the universe of higher mental processes
and began to reflect intelligence - the innate capacity.

Binet (in France) in developing his Scales (1905 1908,
1911) continuously stressed that his tests reflected: ability
or inability to function within the schools of Paris (Binet, 1911;
Pollack and Brener, 1969), further Edwards (1971) stated that
Binet's test was some means to give a current estimate of the
intellectual status of a school-age child, such that his educability could be determined. Although Binet said that it was possible to make comparisons between individuals by using his scale,

he further cautioned that these comparisons should be considered
in their present scope and form, without attempts to define it
as acquired or congenital (Binet and Simon, 1905; Edwards, 1971);
for to do so was beyond the scope of his scale.

Stern (in Germany) who introduced the term IQ as a possible index of brightness expressed from the results of an intelligence test did not claim that the test measured inborn capacity;
he wrote that no series of tests, however skillfully selected it
may be, does reach the innate intellectual endowment, stripped
of all complications, but rather this endowment, in conjunction
with all influences to which the examinee has been subjected up
to the moment of testing (Stern, 1914). Stern further stated
that it was just these external influences that are different in
the lower social classes, and thus higher class children for
various reasons meet the demands of the test better than children
of the uncultured classes.

Decrolyn and Degand (in Denmark) although not stating any
further reflections of the Binet scale; noted a significant finding --- that there were definite social class differences in the
test results (Decrolyn and Degand, 1910). Upon informing Binet
of such a discrepancy in his test, Binet based on empirical studies reached the same conclusion - that the test results reflected
higher scores on the average of one-and one-half years for persons
of superior social classes, when compared with the poorer child
for whom the test was designed (Binet, 1908).

Goddard (in the United States) took only the slightest

modified Binet Scale (Goodenough, 1949) and upon being sure that it was functional with children in the Vineland Schools, and institutionalized Americans, stated that the test reflected innate capacity (Davies, 1959; Pickens, 1968); and showed the superiority of one race over the others; thus lending support for the eugenic philosophy of racial isolation because of the inherent inferiority of some races (Blacks) by comparisons to others (European-Whites).

It would seem, then, that upon being translated into English, crossing the Atlantic Ocean and touching North American (U.S.) soil, suddenly for the first time the "mental test" ceased to reflect a sampling of the universe of higher mental processes and became a reflector of innate capacity. Although this may seem intellectually unacceptable (that by crossing the Atlantic and touching North American soil the test took on a new and obviously different function) it is not impossible to believe: many simi-lar fantastic happenings occurred in crossing that great Atlantic. Black slaves, stolen (or sold) from their ancestoral homeland, upon crossing the Atlantic and touching U.S. soil ceased to be Rousseau's "noble savages" and became sub-human elementary varieties of human species (Davenport, 1972; Goddard, 1911, 1912, 1914). Further, the poor, deprived, inferior of Europe: the socially and even genetically inferior - if an aristocratic-eugenic position is accepted - in that the genetically superior will overcome any disadvantage in his socioeconomic environment and win the positions of status and power in the social order; these European poor had not overcome such ills in the thousands of years they had lived in Europe, upon crossing the Atlantic,

77

touching U.S. soil and melting in this great melting pot, ceased in less than four hundred years to be the inferior of Europe and became the superiors of the world (both socially and genetically). Thus accepting, as fact, that the tests (Goddard's Translation and later Terman's Stanford Revision) of intelligence reflected innate hereditable capacity, simply by being translated into English, crossing the Atlantic and touching U.S. soil is a not at all unreasonable position when comparison is made in the above light.

Terman (again in the United States) took and revised the Binet Scale; introduced and popularized the use of Stern's IQ concept, as an index of brightness derived at through mathematical calculations from a raw score, and gave a standardization procedure which proved the test to be of extreme usefulness in predicting school related abilities (Edwards, 1971). Terman, although cautioning that the test should be used in an educational setting with various limits, accepted the basic notion that the test was reflecting some innate capacity, transmittable through inheritance (Pickens, 1968; Bayley, 1970).

During the next twenty years in America, the Stanford Revision (1916, 1936) of the Binet Scales ceased to be a representation for intelligence --- with many psychologists, sociologists, and especially educators and the lay public; and for many became synonymous with intelligence itself (Goodenough, 1949).

During this expanse of time (1917-1937) group tests were developed for use in the Army and later, after the war, for use with the general population. The various group tests to follow (Pintner-Cunningham, 1938; Revised Army Beta, 1935; Progressive Matrix, 1938; Cattell Culture-Free, 1944; Kuhlman-Anderson, 1927; Otis Group, 1919, etc.) were based, for the most part on the theory that intelligence is a general capacity and should be measured by means of sampling a variety of mental activities (Freeman, 1955), which is basically the theoretical position taken by Binet (Binet, 1908) in devising his various scales. Thus the test materials used on the various group tests were not all new innovations, and had already been employed in the earlier testing movements of both the United States and various European countries (Freeman, 1955). Freeman (1955) further stated that based on a hugh volume by Yerkes, 1921 on the psychological uses of group testing in the army many periodical articles and books appeared on such subjects as racial and national differences in intelligence and not only were many of these data of doubtful validity but some of the interpretations and publications based upon them gave rise to serious misapprehensions (Freeman, 1955).

Wechsler (1939) decided to extend the tests already in use (especially the Stanford-Binet Scale) so as to measure adequately adult intelligence. Wechsler adapted a general-factor theory of intelligence, but decided to use both verbal and non-verbal mate-rials (thus combining items from both the original individual testing movement given impetus by Binet and Simon and those of the performance movement). Wechsler took items and subtests which had been widely used and validated by other psychologists, thus making his scale nothing unique (as far as getting at possible different

and more specific determinants of intelligence). Thus the
Wechsler Scales (1939, 1949, 1955, 1967) reflected basically the
same theoretical position as the scales from which they had been
derived and validated - that being school related abilities
(Binet, 1908; Terman, 1906; Edwards, 1971).

Later performance scales (Pintner-Paterson Scale 1917;
Gesell, 1925; Cattell, 1940) were devised as a supplement to and
substitute for the Stanford-Binet Scale (Freeman, 1955), to be
used with deaf, illiterate or non-English speaking subjects.
These performance scales were basically designed as an extension
downward of the Stanford-Binet Scale (Cattell, 1940); and those
that employed traditional validation procedures, validated by
correlating their measurement techniques (tests) with a test (or
various tests) already in existence. It appears that performance
tests then are simply different ways of getting at basically the
same behavioral universals as the previously existing measurements of mental abilities (intelligence) - specifically the Binet
and Stanford-Binet Scales.

It appears that the present testing techniques employed
in test construction and methodology in the United States have been
derived from and given impetus by Binet's original scale of 1905.
This scale and his others which followed (1908, 1911) were a reflection of: school related abilities and not to be used to get
at any congenital or acquired determination of the deficiencies
reflected in the test results (Binet, 1908; Goodenough, 1949;
Freeman, 1955; Edwards, 1971). The testing movement in America
to follow (Goddard, 1910; Terman 1961; Yerkes, 1915; Wechsler,

1939; Performance Testing, 1917; Group Testing, 1917; etc.) all seem to have build more or less on the basic Binet model (both theoretically and methodologically) and thus the tests as derived and validated against the original and revised Binet scales, did then, and still does, reflect what the Binet scales reflected: higher mental processes presumed to comprise intelligence as it is reflected in a school environment (Binet, 1908; Goodenough, 1949; Edwards, 1971; Zach, 1972), and deficiencies highlighted by test results should be considered in their present scope and form, without attempts to define them as acquired or congenital (Binet and Simon, 1905).

Some few tests of higher mental abilities (intelligence) have been later devised which was not a direct (or slightly modified) outgrowth of Binet's theory and methodology; such tests as culture-free tests and sensorimotor tests of intelligence.

RACE AND INTELLIGENCE

A careful search of the literature since the inception of the first intelligence (or mental) test in France in 1905 reveals literally thousands of articles dealing with race as a determiner of intelligence.

Galton, even before the introduction of tests of mental abilities had predicted that some races were genetically inferior to others (specifically that Black races were inferior to White races - Pintner, 1931). The eugenic movement, both in Britain and the United States, accepted this assumption on the heritability of innate abilities with racial differences (where Blacks were at the lower extreme) as their banner, and much to their surprise found that when a measure of such high mental abilities was at last introduced by Binet in France and translated into English (with only slight modifications - Goodenough, 1949) by one of their own members, H. H. Goddard, it at last confirmed their assumption about the inferiority of certain races.

With the later revision of the Binet Scale by Terman in 1916 further confirmation as to the genetic inferiority of certain races was confirmed and accepted. That the original Binet Scale had been found to show social class differences (Binet, 1908; Decrolyn and Degand, 1910) and that test scores on his own scale showed problems concerning the differences in cultural level of the home from which the child came (Edwards, 1971) seemed to be of limited concern to Terman. He said, that such effects has not been accurately determined, and cited a limited number of cases where most of the children in a family scored relatively low, but one child scored very high - such an incident reduced the strength of the argument about cultural differences, Terman believed (Edwards, 1971).

The research on racial differences and intelligence over the past sixty years has portrayed Blacks (when compared to Whites) as lacking in almost every trait which has been termed higher mental processes. The fact that these mental processes were genetically determined and therefore Blacks were inherently inferior to Whites, although begun by Glaton and the Eugenic movements (world wide) was given further impetus by Arthur Jensen in 1969 (Jensen, 1969).

A sampling of the research showing Black deficiencies (inferiorities) in higher mental capacities as reflected by intelligence testing, include deficiencies in: (1) Physical and Motor Development (Strong, 1913; Sunne, 1917; Meredith, 1943; Brown, Lyon and Anderson, 1945); (2) Psychomotor Development (Chapman, 1944; Covell, 1950); (3) Memory (Phillips, 1914); (4) Language (Arlitt, 1922; Hewitt, 1930; Bernstein, 1960; Cazden, 1968; Brensnaker and Blum, 1971); (5) Home Environment (Farr, 1931; Bousfield, 1932; Johnson, 1954; Clark, 1965; Kennedy, Havighurst, and Eels, 1963);

(6) Logical Analysis (Peterson, 1923; Sunne, 1925; Graham, 1926; Patrick and Sims, 1934); (7) Personality Development (Rowntree, 1943; Pollack, 1944; Hunt, 1947; Ripley and Wolfe, 1947; Moses, 1947; Boykin, 1957); (8) Overall Mental Growth (Lacy, 1926; Trabue, 1919; Collum, 1937; Tomlinson, 1944; Jensen, 1969; Herrnstein, 1971); and (9) General Intelligence (IQ) (Boots, 1926; Kock and Simmons, 1926; Clinton, 1931; Pintner, 1931; Bean, 1942); to cite only a few.

The mid-fifties saw a basic refutation to this deficit model to Black intellectual development; although a few researchers at earlier dates had argued against this deficit model. Research on the same areas as mentioned above to refute this deficit model to Black intelligence include: (1) Physical and Motor Development (Rhoads, Rapoport, Kennedy and Stokes, 1941; Scott, Cardozo, Smith and DeLilly, 1950); (2) Psychomotor Development (Moore, 1942; Pasamanick, 1946; Woisika, 1944; Irwin, 1949); (3) Memory (Arlitt, 1922; Derrick, 1920); (4) Language (Entwisle, 1968; Valinetine, 1972); (5) Home Environment (Valinetine, 1971); (6) Personality Development (Gardner and Aaron, 1946; Diggs, 1950; Auld, 1952; Kephart, 1954; Hoffman and Albizn-Miranda, 1955); (7) Overall Mental Growth (Young and Bright, 1954; Montagu, 1945; Baratz and Baratz, 1971; Steward, 1960); and (8) General Intelligence (IQ) (Davis, 1928; Shimberg, 1929; Graham, 1930; Gartn, 1937; Carrady, 1946).

Only in one area, that of motor development, have Blacks been historically seen to be equal to if not superior to Whites (see above). Binet had included motor skills as one of the lower components of intelligence; although, earlier researchers (Galton, 1894, 1907, 1914; and Wundt following his lead) had used such sensorimotor tasks as sole predictors (measures) of individual differences --- the early interest in mental abilities or intelligence.

The research on areas of deficiency, inferiority, etc. of Blacks related to higher mental processes and the number of articles done in each area is so extensive that only a brief scanning can be undertaken in this paper. However, it is felt that such a limited listing will show that to many researchers the idea of the genetic (inherent) inferiority of Blacks was generally accepted until about the mid nineteen fifties, when it began to be questioned and re-evaluated by more adequate (or at least more modern) empirical methods.

However, with Jensen's article of 1969 in the Harvard Educational Review, the age old questions on the nature-nurture controversy were again arisen. Jensen, although accepting the basic behavioristic assumption that intelligence is predetermined, with the possibility of enriching or thwarting intelligence by manipulating the environment further postulated that Blacks are inferior to Whites and that the explanation lay in the genes (a position held earlier by many psychologists, sociologists, anthropologists, educators, and a basic eugenic philosophy).

Jensen's now famous article of 1969 appears to be a declaration of war on social scientists who discount man's genetic intellectual heritage (Menecker and Pollack, 1974). As Jensen stated, "the possible importance of genetic factors in racial behavioral differences has been greatly ignored, almost to the point of being tabooed." Early in his article one is able to get a hint of Jensen's preconceived notion as to the causes of racial differences - that being genetics. He quotes Edward L. Thorndike as saying, "In the actual race of life, which is not to get ahead, but to get ahead of somebody, the chief determining factor is heredity," and believed that the evidence concerning intelligence has proved Thorndike correct. Although Jensen believed that the research proved that intelligence is genetically based, he felt that genetic factors in individual differences have usually been obscured, belittled, or degraded. He states, "Fortunately we are beginning to see some definite signs that this mistreatment of the genetic basis of intelligence by social scientists may be on the wane, and that a biosocial view of intellectual development more in accord with the evidence is gaining greater recognition," (Jensen, 1969). Eysenck (1971) one of Jensen's proponents, states that all the evidence to date suggests the strong and indeed over-whelming importance of genetic factors in producing the great variety of intellectual differences which we observe in our culture, and much of the differences observed between certain racial groups. Jensen himself was not so forceful in his assertions, he state that various lines of evidence, none of which is definitive alone, make it a not unreasonable hypothesis that genetic factors are strongly implicated in the average Black-White intelligence difference (Jensen, 1969). Pickens (1968) stated that with the decline of Galtonian eugenics during the late nineteenth century, because of developments in twentieth century science; and the eugenicists discounting of man's behavioral plasticity, a new form of eugenics emerged - incorporating the latest social and scientific theories. Contemporary eugenics, he states, no longer has the anti-environmental bias of their Galtonian forerunners; and as far as class prejudice, eugenicists of today do not provide psuedobiological rationales for existing distinctions in power and wealth. A more balanced view of man's behavior - the complexity of social-genetic relationship in human nature - has resulted (Pickens, 1968; Ginzberg, 1956; Goodsell, 1938). As an example Pickens (1968) states that the modern eugenicist no longer stresses hereditary determinism. Today their position is that the organism has a hereditary tendency that under a certain environmental situation might find expression. Jensen and his followers (Herrnstein and Shockley) appear to have taken a modern eugenic approach to viewing racial differences in America. Jensen states, that genetic and environmental factors should not be viewed as being in opposition to each other, nor are they an all or none affair. Jensen believes that the legitimate question is not whether the characteristic is due to heredity or environment, but what proportion of the population variation in the characteristic is attributable to genotypic variation and what proportion is attributable to non-genetic or environmental variation in the population. Using studies of monozygotic twins reared together, Jensen states that 75% of the variance in IQ is due to genetic variation and 25% to environmental variation.

It has often been argued that since we cannot really measure intelligence, we cannot possibly determine its heritability.

According to Jensen, whether intelligence can be measured or not makes no difference to the question of heritability. We do not estimate the heritability of some trait that lies hidden behind our measurements. We estimate the heritability of the phenotypes and these are the measurements themselves. If the test scores get at nothing genetic, the result will simply be that estimates of their heritability will not differ significantly from zero. The fact that heritability estimates based on IQs differ very significantly from zero is proof that genetic factors play a part in individual differences in IQ (Jensen, 1969).

But then, how can a socially defined attribute, such as intelligence, be said to be inherited? Jensen states, that the brain mechanisms which are involved in learning are genetically conditioned just as are other structures and functions of the organism. What the organism is capable of learning from the environment and its rate of learning, thus have a biological basis (Jensen, 1969).

Jensen, Shockley and Herrnstein further suggested eugenics to be part of the solution to the intelligence-heredity problems. Shockley has proposed a program of sterilization to combat what he calls dysgenics, the breeding of inferior genetic stock. In an interview published in The Harvard Crimson, Herrnstein recommended gathering IQ information as part of the U.S. census, so that we could observe dysgenic trends in American society. Asked what such information could be used for, Herrnstein replied: "If at some time in the future we decide that our population is getting too large, and we need to limit it, we could use census information on IQ to decide how and when to limit it" (Herrnstein, 1971).

In his article of 1969, Jensen wondered: If there is a danger that current welfare policies, unaided by eugenic foresight, could lead to the genetic enslavement of a substantial segment of our population. It appears to be evident from the afore-mentioned testimonies, that eugenic sterilization has moved from the physiological (i.e., insane, epileptic, feebleminded) to behavioral; with many elements of society feeling that its ills may possibly be due to genetic or biological problems of individuals or groups of individuals - with some possible racial undertones. The questions arise: Who will control dysgenics of a social nature? Who has the authority to decide which genes are defective and which behavior abnormal? We must become more aware that the application of science is not merely a scientific concern but a political and social issue as well.

Of all the research on race and intelligence which has portrayed Blacks as lacking in (or deficient, deprived, inferior, etc.) all higher mental processes, less than one half of one percent of the more than 1000 articles of comparisons between Blacks and Whites surveyed by this author could be found where the Black race was not in actuality a suppressed Black ethnic minority, within a larger White (more specifically Anglo-Saxon) society. The majority of the studies cited in the literature were done in England (Robson, 1931; Oliver, 1931; Loades, 1917; Nessen, 1934), the United States (Shuey, 1958, 1966; Dreger and Miller, 1960; Kennedy, Keitt and White, 1963), South Africa (Martin, 1915), and Australia (Teasdale, 1968; Porteus, 1917). A limited number of the research articles were done in island colonies of these various countries; specifically Jamacia (Davenport, 1928), Hawaii (Porteus, 1930) and other studies done in India (Herrick, 1921). Thus it appears that these various countries all have (or have had) extremely suppressed Black ethnic minorities, and it is professed that maybe such studies were simply man's strivings to justify his social ills, or as Pickens (1968) puts it, "Galton's creed meet the psychic needs of progressive America with its status crisis."

Few, if any, racial studies dealing with the effects of race on intelligence have been done; for the sole reason that like intelligence, race (as it has been used in the scientific research) is a poorly defined term. Race is a biological concept with racial identification established by means of biological characteristics of the individual which are transmitted to him genetically from his forebearers. (McDavid and Harari, 1968, 1974; Boas, 1929; Klineberg, 1935; Benedict, 1943; Pickens, 1968). There are three conventionally accepted racial groups: (a) Mongoloids (yellow-skinned Asiatics), (b) Negroids (black-skinned Africans and Pacific groups), and (c) Caucasoids (white-skinned Europeans). Certain anthropologists have argued that the history of known migrations cannot account for the geographic distribution of these categories over the earth, and have thus proposed a minimum of eleven necessary racial classifications (Coon, Garn and Bridsell, 1950). Even these classifications are crude in establishing reliable scientific criteria for defining the biological concept of race. Skin color does not provide discrete categories for racial classification, since skin color ranges from charcoal black to albino white - with a variety of browns, tans, and yellows; and can be found in almost every race --- also skin shade may be modified through disease, diet and environmental effects. Eye colors provide no discretely defined categories because the range is too limited; with dark eyes characterizing all racial classifications except the white-skinned Caucasian, who occationally show hazel or blue eyes. Nor does blood group classification show any promise as a basis for biological classification, since frequencies of blood types have been found to be distributed among all racial groups. Other anthropometric indices have been proposed (or used) in racial classifications, including: measures of physical form of the human body; head size; size of chest and trunk; length of limbs; amount, quantity, texture and distribution of hair over the body - to name only a few (McDavid and Harari, 1968, 1974). A combination of these various characteristics have been used in reaching the three conventionally accepted classifications of race.

That such is not biologically sufficient to determine race as it affects determinants of human behavior (be they intelligence, aggression, or whatever) should be made even more obvious when one examines the inconsistencies for defining race. In the United States, convention decrees that an individual who has one Negro great-grandparent (i.e., one-eighth Negro) should be classified as Negro. On the contrary, the individual with one White great-grandparent (i.e., one-eighth White) is not classified as White (McDavid and Harari, 1968, 1974). That Blacks in the United States are genetically identical (or even statistically similar) to Aborigines

91

of Australia or Zulus of South Africa should be a questionable assumption (especially if one accepts the assumption that race is
the result of geographical or social isolation of one group from
another for several generations - Boas, 1929; Dunn, 1967; Pickens,
1968, and the extreme hybridization of the Black population in
the United States).

Even when racial identification is clearly recognized to
be biologically defined, McDavid and Harari (1968, 1974) have said
it is often still difficult for the scientists to establish racial
membership conclusively, this being due to the fact that the human
species is highly hybridized and interbred. Relatively few individuals are of truly pure genetic stock, and it is almost impossible to trace specific strains in human beings.

What then has most of the research on racial determinants
of intelligence actually sampled if not race? This author professes that what the various researchers have tapped were (are)
ethnic differences between groups and their effects on human
development (intelligence more specifically) in combination with
various other variables.

Ethnicity is a sociological concept with ethnic identification established by examination of the society (including its
customs, its conventions, and its socialization practices) of
which the individual is a member (McDavid and Harari, 1968, 1974).
McDavid has stated that most people who are behavioral scientists
(and even occasionally a careless behavioral scientist) confuse
the concepts of race and ethnicity; although the two are not

parallel. This author professes that far too often have even the behavioral scientists confused the two concepts (especially in light of the multiplicity of research in the scientific journals).

In America the fact that many members of the minority populations may not have the same effective culture - the culture which actually impinge on and affect individuals and/or groups within the larger culture (McCandless and Evans, 1973) as the majority (White middleclass) population (Valinetine, 1971, 1972) has added to the already difficult task of isolating racial and ethnical bases of behavior and has limited our scientific knowledge of the contribution of race to the determination of human behavior (McDavid and Harari, 1968, 1974).

Another significant factor which has interacted with race and ethnicity in the early (and present) studies attempting to ascertain racial determinants of intelligence has been that of socioeconomics. Socioeconomics (or social class) factors were definitely shown to affect mental test scores (Binet, 1908; Decrolyn and Degand, 1910; Edwards, 1971). For many years the greater percentage of Blacks in America comprised the lower socioeconomic (social class) level; so much so that Black (or Negro) became synonymous with poor or lower class. The fact that Blacks comprised the lower socioeconomic classes and mental tests as devised by Binet (and translated and revised by Goddard and Terman) showed lower scores for poorer classes, and more recently that Blacks have (and have had) a different environment (culturally, linguistically, etc.) with Binet, Stern and others saying that the

93

culture of the child may affect his score on mental tests has raised many questions concerning accepting the assumption that intelligence test scores (Stanford-Binet Revision, Binet Scales, or any other scale which has not been developed and standardized for that specific group) reflect some innate genetically inheritable capacity for the Black populations (or any minority population for whom the tests were not devised and standardized or which has items which are more or less difficult for certain segments within the population).

MODELS OF SOCIALIZATION AND THE BLACK CULTURE IN AMERICA -
AN INTRODUCTION

Definitions of socialization vary from lengthy and abstract paragraphs to terse statements about human behavior; however, these variations in definitions are more the result of idiosyncratic motives than differing epistimological notions (Sorokin, 1956).

Kimball Young (1949) defines socialization as an interactional relationship by means of which the individual learns the social and cultural requirements that make him a functioning member of his society. Child (1954) considers socialization to be the whole process by which an individual, born with behavior potentialities of an enormously wide range, is led to develop actual behavior which is confined within a much narrower range - the range of what is customary and acceptable for him according to the standards of his group. Horton and Hunt (1964) defines socialization as a process by which an individual internalizes the norms of his groups so that a distinct "self" emerges, unique to that individual. Roucek (Fairchild, 1968) sees socialization as a sociopsychological process whereby the personality is created under the influence of the educational institutions; a process intertwined with: (a) the institutions wherein the general conditioning process relates itself to the school process, the family, play groups, racial groups, community, church, motion pictures and the like - and with (b) some problems of the sociology of groups formed in the educational process, and of the groups engaged in education.

More simply, socialization has been defined as the integration of an organism into an ongoing social system (McDavid and Harari, 1968, 1974). This social system can be of many kinds - such as a club, a church, fraternity or sorority, one's peer group, etc. What appears to be of more significance in the present discussion (and thus the definition used for socialization in this paper) is the integration of a child into his ongoing culture.

Socialization has thus been said to be a descriptive, value ridden, culturally and developmentally relativistic lay term that ill meets the requirements for a rigorous definition demanded by science (Reese and Lipsitt, 1970). That cultural and developmental relativism operate importantly in evaluating socialization is clear: The "get-up-and-go" considered desirable in a North American (U.S.) ten year old female would be considered, at the very least, as being in bad taste for a well-reared girl in a conventional middle class Japanese family. The openness of heterosexual behavior permitted in Margaret Mead's (1928) Samoa would, if detected, put a North American (U.S.) boy or girl in Juvenile Court. The curious, questioning, spontaneously vocal third grader in a progressive demonstration school would be considered intolerably aggressive and out of line in a conventional, authoritarian school system. The angry physical encounters considered normal in a group of two year olds would be severely put down among fifth grade children. The vigorous verbal sexiness of a lower class elementary school boy constitutes disturbed behavior if shown by a middle class girl (Reese and Lipsitt, 1970).

That a scientist holds values is nothing for which to apologize - but a scientist must be extremely careful that his values do not influence the way in which he gathers, analyzes, interprets, and generalizes from his data. Reese and Lipsitt (1970) thus conclude that no absolute definition, but only a relativistic definition of socialization can be provided, and that to evaluate any child's socialization on a good-bad or effective-ineffective dimension, one must consider at the very minimum the following variables: (a) the generally accepted ways of behaving within the child's effective culture, (b) sex, (c) chronological, mental, and physical age and (d) social class. They say that some other researchers would like to include race as an important element in the socialization process (in America) but conclude that not enough research has been done to draw such a conclusion -- thus racial variables are included under their social class heading.

The possibility that Blacks in the United States may function in a different culture (whether effective and/or formal) has brought about much provocative research since about the mid-nineteen sixties. This research has lead to the formulation of the Difference and Bicultural models of Black socialization, as alternatives to the commonly held Deficit model. The deficit hypothesis to cognitive (as well as language, social, etc.) development

97

professes that Black children are cognitively (and otherwise) deficient due to genetics (Jensen, 1969; Herrnstein, 1971) or due to environmental effects associated with slavery, poverty and discrimination (Havighurst and Breese, 1947; Eels, et al, 1951; Clark, 1965; Kennedy, et al, 1963). The difference hypothesis to cognitive development professes that Black children have developed different styles of cognition, language, etc. as a result of being socialized in an ethnically different culture (Baratz and Shuy, 1969; Steward, 1962, 1964, 1965, 1966, 1968) and the bicultural model of cognitive (social, language, etc.) development suggest that Blacks are socialized into two cultures at the same time; one the result of being a part of a different ethnic group and the other the result of having to cope (in schools, work situations, and otherwise) with the dominate middle class White culture (Valentine, 1968, 1971, 1972; Polgan, 1960).

Deficit Model

The deficit hypothesis of cognitive (or psychological) development of Blacks appears to have had its inception in what could be termed a Western-European interpretation of anthropological, sociological and psychological thought. That is, many sociologists argue as to whether the ancient Greeks (especially) and other ancient peoples had what could be termed a science of sociology - or if simply they had what could be termed social thought (Gittler, 1941). Thus arguments arose that sociology (and very similarly anthropology and psychology) originated: (1) in the seventeenth and eighteenth centuries (professed by Sombart, Brinkmann and Tonnies); (2) that sociology began in the romantic period of about 1800 (Small, von Below, and Baxa) and (3) that the nineteenth century is the period which gave rise to sociology (Barth, Oppenheimer, H. Weber, Gothein, Freyer, Squillace, von Stein and von Mohl - Gittler, 1941). No matter which of these periods one accepts for the origins of sociological (anthropological and psychological) thoughts vs. social thought, one would have to note the Western-European brand stamped thereon - that is: social thought can hardly be considered a science or a discipline. A science (sociology, anthropology, and psychology) must possess a body of knowledge, theories, and generalizations - and it was not until at the earliest the seventeenth century and at the latest the nineteenth century that such an empirical gathering of knowledge was undertaken. Further, this Western-European attitude having already been heavily influenced by Social Darwinism, Mendelian and Galtonian Theories, the Eugenic movement and a generally accepted assumption that they (Europeans) were the superior living humans --- as exemplified in the vast democratic social systems they had cre-ated and maintained over the centuries.

This deficit theory of Black socialization took strong roots in America and as early as the 1950s there were reports of the disadvantaged child in the ghetto, and early studies as to the inadequacies of the Black mother-child interaction process. Also during the early 1960s many books and articles were written to awaken interest in this disadvantaged culture (Conant's Slums and Suburbs, 1961; Reissman's The Culturally Deprived Child, 1962; K. Clark's Dark Ghetto, 1965 and Fantini and Weinstein's The Dis-advantaged - Challenge to Education, 1968; to name only a few).

A prime example of this deficiency hypothesis has always been seen in the area concerning verbal skills of the Black ghetto resident. This position has been beautifully summarized by P. Dale (1972): "Because Negro children from the ghetto hear very little language, much of it ill formed, they are impoverished in their means of verbal expression and reception. They cannot formulate complete sentences; they speak in 'giant-words.' They do not know the names of common objects, they lack crucial concepts, and they cannot produce or comprehend logical statements. Sometimes they are even reported to have no language at all." Nothing could be farther from the truth - probably no group in America is more verbal than the Black ghetto resident.

As a result of these and many similar accounts of the Black community, the passage of the 1954 Desegregation Act, and an interest on the part of the Johnson Administration; Moynihan was commissioned to study and find causes for this disadvantage in the Black community. The Moynihan report (1964) concluded that the Black culture was matriarchal and thus out of "kilt" with the White patriarchal society in America. William Coleman was commissioned in 1964 to study the inequalities in the American schools and to report back to the Commissioner of Education. In 1966, Coleman gave a report on "Equality and Educational Opportunity," which came to be known as the Coleman report. This report lay dormant for several years - but with Jensen's article of 1969 being supposedly based on data from the Coleman report, new impetus and much research using Coleman data as its basis was initiated.

The great majority of these early studies (and books) took the position that something was wrong with the Black community which was causing Blacks not to be able to measure up to the normal population in America (meaning White middle class population). Conant (1961) saying that the Black family was the cause of this problem and that the problems were more socioeconomic than racial (later McDavid and Harari, 1968, 1974; and Reese and Lipsitt, 1970 have taken this position). Moynihan (1964) saying that the Black community was a matriarchal society and thus out of harmony when compared to the patriarchal American society; and Kenneth Clark (1965) saying that the causes of this deficiency were due to poverty, segregation and related circumstances and not to deficits within the family unit.

Another school was composed of those who felt that the reasons for the deficits in the Black community were due to genetic (or inherited) factors. Jensen (1969 and earlier the Eugenicists) giving impetus to this movement and stating that 75% intelligence (cognitive development) was due to heredity, while only 25% was due to environmental and other factors; further Jensen assumed that Blacks were genetically inferior to Whites in intelligence. Shockley and Hernstein took Jensen's report (a modern eugenic position) and carried it to the extreme original eugenic position, stating that the genetically superior would always be cognitively more developed than the genetically inferior (or that Whites would always be genetically superior to Blacks) and that we were presently contaminating the genetic pool of mankind by allowing the genetically inferior (Blacks) to breed with the genetically superior (Whites).

The deficit hypothesis of development was not only profound in research on cognitive development of Black children but branched out into other areas. In the area of cognitive styles, much research has been done to show that lower socioeconomic Black children and their parents are more impulsive than middle class children and their parents (Kagan and Kogan, 1970; Hess and Shipman, 1965; Debus, 1968); lower class children are more field dependent than middle class children (Cohan, 1965; Bieri, 1960) - where reflexivity and field independence are considered more cognitively developed. Studies suggesting lower socioeconomic (Black) children are less (deficient) achievement motivated (Kagan and Moss, 1969; Katz, 1967); lower class children have in a similar way been shown to be lower in all of these traits which pertain to higher mental processes.

By believing that Black children are deficient in language skills we have not admitted to the existence (or possible existence) of their having a different language and thus have constantly taught Black children in what may be a foreign language to them. By insisting on a deficit hypothesis we have suggested earlier and earlier intervention into the child's life, so much so, that we may suggest as Bettelheim (1943) the taking away of the child from his mother; when we know the drastic effects of such, even if the mother is maladjusted (Goldfart, 1943, 1945; Levy, 1947; Skeels, 1966). By adhering to the deficit hypothesis we insist that the school system remain the same for Black children, even when we see that schools are failing (especially for Black children) (Fantani and Young, 1968; Holt, 1964, 1967); and finally by insisting on the deficit hypothesis we present the Black child as a sick White child, thus lowering his self-image and his self-esteem, increasing his fear of failure and in essence insuring his inferior position in our society.

The Difference Model

The cultural difference model of Afro-American socialization could be said to have been given impetus by Franz Boas and the social anthropology movement about the early 1930s (Putnam, 1961). Further impetus was given by the research on whether intelligence testing is culturally biased against the Black child (Kennedy, 1963; Havighurst, Davis, Haggard, Eels, 1948, 1953) whether Black children achieve in other than academic areas (McCandless, 1967) whether language was in fact different for Black children (Labov, 1971; Valentine, 1971, 1972). Other synonyms for this model of development include cultural pluralism, cultural diversity and generally a multicultural approach to viewing the socialization process in America. This cultural difference hypothesis recognizes that differences are not necessarily deficiencies and indeed have enriched the lives of all Americans, by contributing (through the melting pot theory) to the American way of life. Here the basic assumptions are that all children, regardless of their ethnic origin, are similar in their basic needs; yet, children of various national and ethnic origins are also significantly different. J. D. Grambs (1960) highlighted the problems inherent in such conditions by stating that we know from examining American life that differences among groups and individuals are often the sources of conflicts and tensions, within our society.

The difference model is in direct opposition to the deficit model in almost every way of viewing Black socialization; with research on Black language being probably the most articulated and abundant. Many sociologists, anthropologists, dialectologists, psychologists, etc. have argued that the non-standard English of many Blacks in the United States is by no means a direct descendant of British English - but rather is the product of language contact between many African dialects and English; and that because of racial isolation and the American caste system, Black English has remained a systematic and intact language which has phonological, morphological and syntactic similarities and differences which set it apart from Standard English (Bryen, 1974; Labov, 1967; Valentine, 1971, 1972).

The deficit hypothesis of Black English although the most challenged hypothesis by those persons supporting a difference theory to Afro-American socialization is by no means the only form of the socialization process challenged by these theorists. The research since the mid-nineteen fifties especially seem to challenge all phases of the deficit hypothesis to the Black experience.

Some psychologists, among them Kenneth Clark, have argued that this difference hypothesis is simply another way to discriminate against the Black minority especially, and other minorities

in general, in America. These psychologists profess that it has
always been the philosophy of the American (U.S.) society that
differences existed between the mainstream culture (White middle
class) and the various minority subcultures; and that the way to
eliminate these differences (which in essence were seen as deficiencies) was to melt away the minority characteristics into the
larger societal characteristics. Thus Clark (1965-74) and others
have argued that a return to the teaching and encouragement of
differences will also be a return to discrimination and alien-
ation of those who are different. The effects of returning, accepting and teaching a difference theory to socialization in
America which Clark was alluding to, are understandable; however,
it is professed that to do so is a necessity if the Black (and
other minority) ethnic subcultures are to be completely accepted
by and into the mainstream culture. A return to differences -
where differences are seen as such and appreciated, accepted,
honored and cherished by those who are different (as well as all
elements of the society) is necessary. Like almost all other proud
cultures (even though different) once fate has thrust them together -
a new culture has been formed which is a compilation of the best
of the two formal cultures; and a culture with which members of
each of the previous cultures can identify fully.

The Bicultural Model

The Bicultural model to Black socialization is the most recent of the three models; and probqbly can be traced in America to early work by Polgan (1960) when he applied the process of bi-culturation - the process of simultaneously learning behavior patterns from two recognizedly separate ways of life (Valentine, 1972). Polgan found that Indians living on reservations went through a dual process; they learned not only their own culture but that of the mainstream (White) culture as well. Operating from the hypothesis that there exists a separate Black culture, the pro-ponents of this theory profess that it is conceivable that Blacks in America would also go through a similar process labeled bi-culturation.

Accepting the assumption that there is a unique Black culture, then the collective behavior and social life of the Black community is bicultural in the sense that each Afro-American ethnic segment draws upon both a distinctive repertoire of standardized Afro-American group behavior and, simultaneously, patterns derived from the mainstream cultural system of Euro-American derivation (Valentine, 1971). Socialization into both cultures begins at birth and continues throughout life. Both cultures are of varying importance in the lives of most individuals in the Black community; with the ghetto culture more pronounced during early childhood and varying later depending on the degree to which the child wants (and is encouraged) to participate in the mainstream culture.

To better understand the concept of double ethnic identities within a larger social system, one must ask, why cultural differences should persist? R. S. Bryce-Laporte, a West Indian, did a study of his own people living in the U.S. Panama Canal Zone. He described the Canal Zone as a colonial, conflict-based plural system, a two caste system in which Afro-Americans are denied economic access, social status, and political power to control the social determinants of their fate (Valentine, 1972). Bryce-Laporte asked the question, why cultural differences should persist, and even so why they should persist when the subordinate group is constantly exposed to the culture of the dominant elite? The fact that the Black people living in the area are totally dependent in a closed, single-authority system, and are therefore always living on the brink of a crisis, is the basis for his answer. He concludes that living under these conditions Black Panamians regard the dominant culture as foreign, false, and formal, and their culture as natural and normal. In such a situation Bryce-Laporte says the minority culture develops for its self protection a contraculture --- a distinctive pattern which enable the dominated group to adapt to crisis conditions through both their traditional institutions and any new institutions they may develop by way of social movements for change (Valentine, 1972).

In order to survive in a hostile society, it is conceivable that the oppressed Afro-American culture in the United States had to learn to manipulate the dominant culture and also, maintain its own distinctive behavior patterns. Looking from this perspective, it becomes clear that Afro-Americans survived by developing a divided identity consciousness; they had not only to be aware of the dual cultural systems, but had to be able to function in both worlds according to the different standards of each. The Afro-American had also to be willing to receive and accept the Euro-American standards, values, beliefs, and habits if he were to survive - yet he could not accept too much these Euro-American standards; for to do so would alienate him from his own people while not affording him complete access to the mainstream culture - thus a person with no social identity.

Because of segregation and discrimination most Afro-Americans only passively learned the Euro-American standards. In fact, most Black Americans have actually been prevented from completing their life long socialization process into the White culture. They are usually reduced to move to the outer edges of the system. This has been suggested as the reason for an uneducated Black man's ability to understand the complex and technical maneuvers inside a court room, but if called to the witness stand, cannot express himself in a manner in which the attorney, judges, and juries will understand.

There are many problems associated with this bicultural approach to Black socialization. In theory, when the Afro-American becomes socialized into the White culture, he accepts with this the concepts, judgments, and values of that culture. These include viewing other (lower socioeconomic) Blacks with contempt, fear, and hatred. This is what the nationalistic and radical Black is referring to when he talks about the brain washing of his people. Improper socialization in this dual process could produce self hatred and lower self-concept, resulting in a lack of ambition and a complete dissatisfaction with life.

Thus it is possible that an even more complete multi-cultural socialization should be promoted. The socialization process should encourage and teach that differences in ethnicity have completely equal standing when cultural comparisons are made. When all cultures involved in the American way of life are seen as proud, equal and complete cultures --- all existing because they are natural, healthy and beautiful --- then the American dream of "one nation, with liberty and justice for all" can be achieved. Through the melting of several proud cultures (thrust together by history) one larger core culture may be evolved to encompass the contributions of a wide variety of discrete sub-cultures within it.

SUMMARY

In summary it appears that intelligence tests were originally devised to differentiate between subjects who would be able to succeed in traditional school settings of Paris (Binet and Simon, 1905) with no intention of getting at causes; whether acquired or congenital. Later, with an interest in developmental causes of intelligence, researchers speculated that test results also could be generalized to ascertain the etiology of intelligence (Goddard, 1911, 1912, 1914; Terman, 1906; Yerkes, 1915; etc.). Jensen further purported to have derived at statistically from Coleman data the extent to which tests of intelligence reflect racial (or genetic) differences (75%).

Accepting the assumption that tests of intelligence reflect some innate inheritable capacity, which many psychologists, sociologists, anthropologists, educators, past and present eugenicists, etc. have suggested leaves much reason for speculation. This author professes that such people have failed to take their assumption to its logical conclusion --- and purposes to do so here.

If we accept the assumption of the supposed reflection of innate inheritable capacities by present tests of intelligence, then we must conclude that subjects making lower scores on such tests are genetically inferior to subjects scoring higher on such tests. This is a position which we have more or less accepted in the past --- and a basis of Jensen's conclusions. Since we find that the poorer (lower and middle) class subjects score on the average below superior (upper) class subjects, both Black and White (Binet, 1908; Decrolyn and Degand, 1910), then we must conclude that lower and middle-class subjects are genetically inferior to upper-class subjects. This is basically an aristocratic approach to heritability (Ford, 1949) and is in essence what many people, scientists and otherwise have professed (Darwin, Glaton, Royality the world-over, the Eugenicists, White and Black Supremacists, etc.). If we look at American history we will see that America was settled by, for the most part, the poor and downtrodden of Europe (the genetically inferior, if this same aristocratic position coupled with eugenic philosophy is accepted), and therefore, the Euro-American population (the results of a melting of European poor) are the most genetically inferior of the European population (or at least among the most genetically inferior).

If the same logic is continued and the eugenic assumption that all non-White races are genetically inferior to all White races is accepted (Goddard, 1911, 1912, 1914, Pickens, 1968) then the conclusion that Black Americans are inferior to the most genetically inferior of the European peoples is reached. Further, adhering to Darwinian Theory of the survival of the fittest (Darwin, 1896) we must conclude that since Black Americans were the ones who were weakest (in that they lost the battles for survival and were sold into slavery by others of their kind, or stolen from their ancestorial homeland - Aron, 1968); then Blacks are among the most genetically inferior of the Black world.

Since the time period involved --- 400 years of American history, and even less time given migratory history of the American population --- is not long enough to account for significant changes in the genetic makeup of the population involved (Darwin, 1896), then finally we must conclude that America is a country composed of the most genetically inferior peoples of the world, both Black and White.

Such a conclusion leaves one to wonder - if the most genetically inferior peoples of the world in 400 years can become the best educated, have the most advanced technology, the best life style, and the longest life expectancy among other things; then what can we expect are the limits of man - <u>Maybe Utopia is not impossible after all</u>!

CONCLUSION

(Where are we now, and where are we headed)

On Wednesday, April 23, 1975, CBS Report presented a television debate of issues concerning "The IQ Myth." Several prominent American psychologists addressed the current concerns with
the problems surrounding the concept of IQ which has plagued our
nation for the past century. Professor Leon Kamin of Princeton
and Professor Cronbach of Stanford stated that IQ tests have been
used in our country as a means of justifying racial discrimina-
tions --- beginning with Goddard's introduction of his translation of Binet's test to show that Southeastern Europeans were
genetically inferior to North Europeans, and thus to set quotas for
the number of Southeastern Europeans immigrating into the United
States. Later Goddard used his test to show that Blacks were
genetically inferior to Whites (Goddard, 1911, 1912, 1914). Arthur
Jensen of Berkeley in 1969 concluded that Blacks were genetically
inferior to Whites (based on data collected from intelligence tests
then in use), stating that 75% of the variance in IQs is due to
genetic variation and 25% to environmental variation (Jensen, 1969).
On the television debate, Jensen further stressed this opinion,
stating that he was now more than ever convinced that Blacks are

inferior to Whites, based on research findings and his own personal observations since that time.

Many psychologists in that debate (e.g., Thorndike and Hagen of Columbia; Kagan of Harvard, Cronbach of Stanford and Jane Mercer of Riverside, California) stressed that IQ scores do not measure human intellectual functioning, but rather a limited amount-of talent --- that talent which is necessary for school related work. Of course, this was basically what Binet, the author of the first intelligence test, had stated (Binet and Henri, 1896; Edwards, 1971). Professor Kagan of Harvard further emphasized that the present IQ tests measure only about five or six of the more than one hundred known parts of the brain functioning. Professors Kagan and McCullum, both of Harvard, further stated that because the items on present intelligence tests are based on average middle class values, then these tests have served as self-fulfilling prophecies (i.e., labeling some children as having low intelligence and then insuring that these children remain in such categories).

Early researchers in the area of intelligence testing hypothesized that intelligence was a fixed variable, and remained fixed over the life of an individual (Bayley, 1970). However, this concept was later found to be invalid. Several researchers in the New York area, in recent years have found that when children were given compensatory education, starting at age two and continuing to entrance into the public schools, then IQ gains were retained even through third grade. This was contrary to some of the research before, stating that compensatory education had no long term advantage (Commission on Civil Rights, 1968). These New York researchers found that when compensatory aid was given by visiting the homes of children and both parents and children were given instruction, then compensatory training appear to have more lasting effects. Much research in areas of this nature are presently in process and much more is desperately needed.

June Mercer of Riverside, California was instrumental in showing that present tests of intelligence were biased against lower class subjects (especially Blacks and Mexican-Americans). Because of her work, and that of others, it is no longer professionally acceptable to classify lower socioeconomic students as mentally retarded on the basis of scores received on a single intelligence test --- thus placing that child into special classes for the mentally retarded. Many large urban school districts, with large concentrations of Black students have discontinued the use of across-the-board intelligence testing (Atlanta Public School District, Atlanta, Georgia being one such school district).

In recent years, especially in research during and after 1973, questions addressing the controversy centering around assessing minority group children have surfaced and are being discussed. Questions attacking current tests as being misused to denigrate the dignity of minorities and further used to justify and severely limit their educational and vocational opportunities due to the tests reflecting only middle class values (Oakland, 1973) are beginning to dominate research in school psychological circles.

To many minority members, the use of educational tests has been perceived as an attempt to maintain a racially biased social order and to insure institutionalized practices seen in the disproportionate number of minority children who are assigned to special education classes and are assigned to lower levels within the teaching programs of various schools.

In response to the charges from minority group members, minority professionals in the social sciences, and psychologists and sociologists in general, there has been a great increase in research among those involved with devising and using various tests of intelligence and achievement. School systems, the testing industry, professional organizations, federal and state governments, and numerous individuals have responded to these criticisms in a number of ways. Many school systems with a large number of ethnically different students have drastically curtailed or eliminated the use of such tests (especially intelligence tests) or eliminated the use of norm-referenced tests (e.g., New York City, Chicago, Los Angeles, Houston and Atlanta). Other school systems are sponsoring workshops and conferences to promote greater understanding of important cultural, social, political and economical factors which influence the development of minority group children. While the major national professional associations have been slow in responding to specific issues raised by minority groups and then in a most vague and ineffective manner (e.g., Standards for Educational and Psychological Tests and Manuals, French and Michael, 1966; Ethical Standards of Psychologists, American

Psycholinguists, 1963; Casebook on Ethical Standards of Psychologists, Moore and Hack, 1967) more recent actions of the American Psychological Association seem to realistically address problems of clarifying or resolving these issues (American Psychologists, 1969) the Federal Government through the office of the Equal Employment Opportunity Commission (EEOC) have attacked many of the problems concerned with assessing minority group members. Its Guidelines on Employment Testing Procedures (Brown, 1966); Preschool Testing and Equal Employment Opportunity (Anderson and Rogers, 1970) and Guidelines on Employment Selection Procedures (Federal Register, Volume 35) were presented in an effort to correct discriminatory procedures against minorities which were the results of test biases. Others have attempted to provide direction and to give guidelines to school psychologists and others who have direct responsibilities for assessment of minority children. Within the last three years at least two large conferences have been held to discuss ways in which assessment instruments could be used affirmatively and to try to initiate organized efforts to improve tests and their use with minority groups. A National Conference on Testing in Education and Employment was held at the Hampton Institute, Hampton, Virginia, in April of 1973, in order to share and collect data on problems, practices, and progress in testing minorities in the United States; identify crucial areas for research and development pertaining to minority group assessment; identify research personnel and institutional resources to be used in research and development activities; and identify centers in various parts of the United States which would sponsor conferences devoted to issues regarding assessing minority groups. The First Annual International Multilingual Multicultural Conference, held in April of 1973 in San Diego, considered similar and other issues which involve multilingual children.

In response to demands by minority groups and requests from school systems and professional organizations, the testing industry has been taking a more active role. The industry was actively involved in the National Conference on Testing in Education and Employment (Oakland and Phillips, 1973). Also, companies are revising (e.g. the Stanford-Binet), and developing new Instruments in an effort to make their tests less objectionable and hopefully more useful. In addition, some companies are sponsoring national and regional conferences, in part, to encourage an appropriate use of tests with minority group children. Equally as significant is the work by many persons associated with colleges and universities who, through their research and writing, are attempting to increase both the clarity of our discussion of basic issues and our professional sophistication in utilizing assessment techniques.

Much attention has been directed toward developing culture-fair tests and examining existing instruments in terms of their cultural biases. While attempts to develop culture-fair tests to date have not been successful, interest in this area remains high (Oakland and Phillips, 1973). A number of persons are challenging the traditional definition for judging the cultural fairness of test (e.g., that a test is culturally fair only if there are no differences in mean scores manifested by different racial

(ethnic) and socioeconomic status groups). For example, Darling-
ton (1971) stated that it is impossible to formulate a generally
satisfactory definition of cultural fairness and suggested that
the question "What is cultural fairness?" be replaced by two questions: "What can be said about tests which discriminate among
cultures at various levels?" and "How does one construct or select
a test with an optimum amount of cultural discrimination?"
Thorndike (1971), Cole (1972), Jensen (1970), and Linn (1973) also
have proposed strategies important for re-examining our previously
simplistic notions regarding cultural fairness.

In addition to the efforts within the testing industry, a
number of psychologists, sociologists, and educators are attempting to develop new instruments which may assess more appropriately
the cognitive abilities and behaviors of particular minority group
children.

Research directed toward examining differential patterns
of mental abilities manifested by children from various social
class and ethnic groups continues. These research efforts often
include the development of new scales. For example, in their
study of cultural differences in mental abilities of 6- and 7-year-
old children, Lesser, Fifer, and Clark (1965) were, in part, responding to the needs expressed by school personnel for testing
instruments that were fair and accurate and yielded a broad assessment of abilities of young children from atypical cultural
backgrounds. They attempted to devise tests that would be as
free as possible from any direct class or cultural bias but still
would be an acceptable measure of intellectual traits; in

addition, they attempted to structure a testing situation so as to enable each child to be evaluated under optimal conditions. Their major findings were as follows: (1) Children from different social classes do manifest differences in the absolute level of the four mental abilities (verbal ability, reasoning, numerical facility, and space conceptualization) but do not manifest differences in the patterns among these abilities; (2) children from four racial-ethnic groups (Chinese, Jewish, Negro and Puerto-Rican) manifest differences in both the absolute level of each mental ability as well as in the patterns among these abilities; and (3) social class and ethnicity do interact to affect the absolute level of each mental ability but do not interact to affect the patterns among these abilities. The results of their work and others which examine differences in cognitive abilities have been used to support the deficit hypothesis. Although many psychologists have interpreted these differences as arising from an <u>interaction</u> between heredity and environmentsl factors, the importance of biogenetic factors in governing human characteristics received increased attention in the wake of Jensen's controversial publication <u>How Much can we Boost IQ and Scholastic Achievement</u>.

Cole and Bruner (1971) challenged the inferences typically made regarding cultural differences by stating that ... cultural differences reside more in differences in the situations to which different cultural groups apply their skills than do differences in the skills possessed by the groups in question and that the problem is to identify the range of capacities readily manifested in different groups and then to inquire whether the range is

adequate to the individual's needs in the various cultural settings. From that point of view, cultural deprivation represents
a special case of cultural difference that arises when an individual is faced with demands to perform in a manner inconsistent
with his past cultural experiences. They stated that the present
social context of the United States, the great power of the middle
class has rendered differences into deficits because of middle
class behavior being the yardstick of success. Further they cite
two implications relevant for education: the recognition of the
educational difficulties in terms of differences rather than a
special kind of intellectual disease may alter the student's status
in the eyes of the teacher, and teachers should stop laboring under
the impression that they must create new intellectual structures
and start concentrating on how to get a child to transfer skills
he already possesses to the task at hand.

Glaser (1972) agreed that we must stop treating psychological differences as deficits and should devote our efforts to
adapting educational environments to individuals differences by
providing for a wide range and variety of instructional methods
and materials. Instead of using test results either to admit or
to reject persons into a rigid educational process, test results
should be used to facilitate a match between a child's specific
cognitive styles and academic learning experiences in which he is
engaged.

Thus if the social scientists are to make a beneficial
impact by resolving issues related to racially based biases in

the testing controversy, more affirmative leadership is needed. In the process of devising suitable assessment practices, the social scientists need to admit limitations, but in so doing to define the boundaries of our profession within which we can and should continue to function. The process of defining these boundaries is never easy. Unfortunately, during the last few years, the literature and to an even greater degree the speeches on assessing minority group children often reflect narrow political motives and tend to be decisive (Oakland and Phillips, 1973). Rhetoric must be replaced with a commitment to an emphatic understanding of various viewpoints, to work in concert with others, and, equally important, to evaluate issues on the basis of informed judgment.

With the continuation of these movements in psychological assessment (and the publicity that goes with them, such as that presented on the NBC special report "The IQ Myth,") we may one day move more in the direction of using intelligence tests for what they were originally intended --- to determine the degree to which students will probably succeed in (traditional) school settings, or to determine the best course of education for each student. However, before this can be accomplished, the competent researcher must examine all segments of the population. Too frequently in today's American society only the poor, the hospitalized, and the incarcerated are available as subjects for the researcher. An all-out effort should be made, both on the part of the researchers and the public at large, to avail the normal subject for examination.

Further, it is suggested that researchers must become more sophisticated in defining, and more objective in evaluating, concepts and phenomena so that true comparative research can begin.

Bibliography

American Psychologist, 1969, 24, 637-650.

Anderson, B., and Rogers, M. (eds.), Personal Testing and Equal Employment Opportunity, Washington, D.C.: U.S. Government Printing Office, 1970.

Arlitt, A. H., "The Relation of Intelligence to Age in Negro Children," Journal of Applied Psychology, 1922, 6, 378-384.

Aron, Raymond, Progress and Disillusion, New York: Frederick A. Praeyer, Publishers, 1968.

Auld, F. J., "Influence of Social Class on Personality Test Responses," Psychological Bulletin, 1952, 49.

Ausubel, D. P., "How Reversible are the Cognitive and Motivational Effects of Cultural Deprivation? Implications for Teaching the Culturally Deprived Child," Urban Education I (1964), 16-38. In Education of the Disadvantaged, eds. A. H. Passow, M. Goldberg, and A. J. Tannenbaum, New York: Holt, Rinehart and Winston, 1967, 306-326.

Ausubel, D. P., and Ausubel, P., "Ego Development Among Segregated Negro Children," In Education in Depressed Areas, ed. A. H. Passow, New York: Teachers College Press, Columbia University, 1963, 109-141.

Bean, K. L., "Negro Responses to Verbal and Non-Verbal Test Materials," Journal of Psychology, 1942, 13, 343-353.

Ballard, P. B., Group Tests of Intelligence, London, 1921.

Baratz, Joan C., and Shuy, Roger W., Teaching Black Children to Read, Washington, Center for Applied Linguistics, 1969.

Baratz, Stephen S., and Baratz, Joan C., "Early Childhood Intervention: The Social Science Base of Institutional Racism," Harvard Educational Review, 40, 1970, 1, 29-50.

Benedict, Ruth and Weltfish, G., The Races of Mankind, (Public Affairs Pamphlet No. 85) New York: Public Affairs Commission, 1943.

Bayley, N., "Development of Mental Abilities," In Mussen, Paul H., ed., Carmichael's Manual of Child Psychology, New York, Wiley, 1970.

Bennett, G. K., "Response to Robert Williams," The Counseling Psychologist, 2, 1970.

Bernstein, Basil, "Class, Codes and Control. Volume I. Theoretical Studies Toward a Sociology of Language," Harvard Educational Review, 1973, 43, 2, 298-302.

Bernstein, Basil, "Language and Social Class," (Research Note), <u>British Journal of Sociology</u>, 1960, 11, 271-276.

Bernstein, B., "Social Structure, Language, and Learning," <u>Educational Research</u>, 3 1961, 163-176. In <u>Education of the Disadvantaged</u>, ed. A. H. Passow, M. Goldberg, and A. J. Tannenbaum, New York: Holt, Rinehart and Winston, 1967, 225-244.

Bettelheim, B., "Individual and Mass Behavior in Extreme Situations," <u>Journal of Abnormal and Social Psychology</u>, 1943, 38, 417-452.

Bettelheim, B., <u>Love is not Enough</u>, New York: Free Press, 1950.

Biehler, Robert F., <u>Psychology Applied to Teaching</u>, Houghton, Miffin Company, Boston, 1971.

Bieri, James, "Changes in Interpersonal Perception Following Social Interaction," <u>Journal of Abnormal Social Psychology</u>, 48, 61-68.

Bieri, James, "Parental Identification, Acceptance of Authority and Within-Sex Differences in Cognitive Behavior," <u>Journal of Abnormal and Social Psychology</u>, 1960, 60, 76-79.

Bieri, James, <u>Clinical and Social Judgment: The Discrimination of Behavioral Information</u>, New York, Wiley, 1966.

Binet, A., and Henri, W., "La Psychologie Individuelle," <u>L'Annee Psychologique</u>, 1896, 2. 411-465.

Binet, A., and Simon, Th., "Le Developpement de l'Intelligence Chez les Enfants," L'Annee Psychologique, 1908, 14, 1-94.

Binet, A., and Simon, Th., "Methods Nouevelles Pour le Diagnostic due Niveau Intellectuel des Anormaux," <u>L'Annee Psychologique</u>, 1905, 11, 191-244.

Binet, A., and Simon, Th., <u>The Development of Intelligence in Children</u>, Arno Press, New York Times Company, New York, 1973.

Blitsten, Dorothy R., <u>Human Social Development</u>, College and University Press, New Haven, Connecticut, 1971.

Boas, Franz, <u>Anthropology and Modern Life</u>, George Allen and Unwin Ltd., London, 1929.

Bobertag, O., "A. Binet's Arbeiten uber die Intellektvelle Entwicklund des Schulkindes," <u>Zietschrift Fur Angewandte Psychologie</u>, 1911, 5, 105-123.

Bolton, T. L., "The Growth of Memory in School Children," <u>American Journal of Psychology</u>, Vol. IV, 1892, 362-380.

Boots, W. E., A Study in the Intelligence of White and of Colored Grade School Children, High School Students, and College Freshmen, Unpublished Master's Thesis, University of Wisconsin, 1926.

Boring, E. G., "In Symposium: Intelligence and its Measurement," Journal of Educational Psychology, 1921, 12, 127-133.

Bousfield, M. B., "The Intelligence and School Achievement of Negro Children," Journal of Negro Education, 1932, I, 388-395.

Boykin, L. L., "The Adjustment of 2078 Negro Students," Journal of Negro Education, 1957, 26.

Bronfenbrenner, Urie, Two Worlds of Childhood/U.S. and U.S.S.R., Russell Sage Foundation, New York, 1970.

Brown, W. (Chairman), Guidelines on Employment Testing Procedures, Washington, D.C.: Equal Employment Opportunity Commission, 1966.

Bruning, J. L., and Kintz, B. L., Computational Handbook of Statistics, Scott, Foresman and Company, Glenview, Illinois, 1968.

Buckingham, G., "In Symposium: Intelligence and its Measurement," Journal of Educational Psychology, 1921, 12, 127-133.

Buros, Oscar K., Educational, Psychological and Personality Tests of 1933/34-36, New Brunswick, N.J., Rutgers University, 1935-37.

Buros, Oscar K., The Mental Measurements Yearbook (1938, 1940, 1946, 1955, 1959, 1965 eds.) Highland Park, N.J., Gyphon Press.

Buros, Oscar K., Personality Tests and Reviews: Including an Index to the Mental Measurements Yearbooks, Highland Park, N.J., Gyphon Press, 1970.

Burt, C., "The Evidence for the Concept of Intelligence," British Journal of Educational Psychology, 1955, 25, 158-177.

Carmichael, Leonard, Carmichael's Manual of Child Psychology, Mussen, Paul H., ed., New York, Wiley, 1970.

Canady, H. G., "The Problem of Equating the Environment of Negro-White Groups for Intelligence Testing in Comparative Studies," The Journal of Social Psychology, 17, 1943, 3-15. In The Psychological Consequences of Being a Black American, ed. R. C. Wilcox, New York: John Wiley and Sons, 1971, 89-101.

Canady, H. G., "The Psychology of the Negro," In P. L. Harriman (ed.), The Encyclopedia of Psychology, New York: Philosophical Library, 1946, 407-416.

Cattell, Raymond B., "Confirmation and Clarification of Primary Personality Factors," Psychometrika, 1947, 12, 197-220.

Cattell, Raymond B., _Personality: A Systematic Theoretical and Factual Study_, New York: McGraw-Hill, 1950.

Cattell, Raymond B., _Personality and Motivation: Structure and Measurement_, Yonkers-on-Hudson, New York; World, 1957.

Cattell, Raymond, _The Measurement of Intelligence of Infants and Young Children_, New York: Science Press, 1940, Psychological Corp., 1960.

Cazden, B. B., "Environmental Assistance to the Child's Acquisition of Grammar," _Unpublished Doctoral Dissertation_, Harvard University, 1965.

Cazden, C. B., "Subcultural Differences in Child Language: An Interdisciplinary Review," Merill Palmer Quarterly, 1966, 12, 185-219.

Chapmans, W. P., "Measurements of Pair Sensitivity in Normal Control Subjects and in Psychoneurotic Patients," _Psychometric Med._, 1944, 6.

Child, I. L., "Socialization," In _The Handbook of Social Psychology_, ed. by G. Lindzey, Cambridge: Addison-Wesley Publishing Company, 1954.

Clark, K. B., _Dark Ghetto: Dilemmas of Social Power_, New York: Harper, 1965.

Clinton, R. J., "A Comparison of White and Negro Children: Norms on Mirror-drawing for Negro Children by Age and Sex," _Journal of Educational Psychology_, 1931, 22, 186-190.

Cohen, David K., "Does IQ Matter?" _Commentary_, April, 1972, American Jewish Committee.

Cohen, R. A., "Conceptual Styles, Culture Conflict, and Non-verbal Tests of Intelligence," _American Anthropologists_, 71, 828-856.

Cole, N., "Bias in Selection," ACT Research Report No. 51, Iowa City, Iowa: American College Testing Program, 1972.

Cole, M., and Bruner, J., "Cultural Differences and Inferences About Psychological Processes," _American Psychologist_, 1971, 26, 867-876.

Coleman, J. S., _Equality of Educational Opportunities_, Washington, D.C.: U.S. Department of Health, Education and Welfare, 1966.

Collum, M. C., "Comparative Capacities and Achievements of White Children in Woodville and Negro Children in Ardmore, Oklahoma," _Unpublished Master's Thesis_, University of Oklahoma, 1937.

Colvin, A., "In Symposium: Intelligence and its Measurements," _Journal of Educational Psychology_, 1921, 12, 127-133.

Conant, James B., _Slums and Suburbs_, New York, McGraw-Hill Book Company, 1961.

Coon, C. S., Garn, S. M., and Birdsell, J. B., <u>Races</u>, Springfield, Ill.: C. C. Thomas, 1950.

Courtis, S. A., <u>Courtis Standard Research Tests in Arithmetic</u>, Detroit, Mich., S. A. Courtis Publisher, 1908.

Covell, L. L., "Presbyopia: Comparative Observations of White and Negro Populations," <u>American Journal of Ophtol.</u>, 1950, 33.

Dale, D., "Structure and Function," <u>Language Development</u>, 1972.

Davenport, Charles B., <u>Heredity in Relation to Eugenics</u>, Arno Press and the New York Times, New York, 1972.

Davenport, C. B., "Race Crossing in Jamaica," <u>Scientific Monthly</u>, 1928, 27, 225-238.

Davenport, Charles B., and Steggerda, Morris, <u>Race Crossing in Jamaica</u>, Westport, Conn., Negro University Press, 1970.

Davies, Stanley P., <u>The Mentally Retarded in Society</u>, New York, Columbia University Press, 1959.

Davis, A., and Havighurst, R. J., "Social Class and Color Differences in Child Rearing," <u>American Sociological Review</u>, 1946, 11.

Davis, R. A., Jr., "Some Relations Between Amount of School Training and Intelligence Among Negroes," <u>Journal of Educational Psychology</u>, 1928, 19, 127-130.

Decroly, O., and Degand, J., "La Mesue de l'Intelligence Chez les Enfants Normaux d'apres les Tests de Binet et Simon: Nouvelle Contribution Critique," <u>Archives de Psychologie</u>, 1910, 9, 81-108.

Decroly, O., and Degand, J., "Les Tests de Binet et Simon pour le Mesure de l'Intelligence: Contribution Critique," <u>Archives de Psychologie</u>, 1906, 6, 27-130.

Derner, G. F., Aborn, M. and Canter, A. H., "The Reliability of the Wechsler-Bellevue Subtests and Scales," <u>Journal of Counseling Psychology</u>, Vol. 14, 1950.

Derrick, S. M., "A Comparative Study of the Intelligence of Seventy-five White and Fifty-five Colored College Students by the Stanford Revision of the Binet-Simon Scale," <u>Journal of Applied Psychology</u>, 1920, 4, 316-329.

Diggs, Mary H., "Some Problems and Needs of Negro Children as Revealed by Comparative Delinquency and Crime Statistics," <u>Journal of Negro Education</u>, 1950, 19.

Dobzhansky, Theodosuis, <u>Evolution, Genetics and Man</u>, New York, Wiley, 1955.

Dobzhansky, T., Evolutionary Biology, New York, Appleton-Century-Crofts, 1967.

Dobzhansky, T., Heredity and the Nature of Man, New York, Harcourt, Brace and World, 1964.

Dobzhansky, T., Genetics and the Origin of Species, 3rd ed., New York, Columbia University Press, 1941.

Dobzhansky, T., Mankind Evolving, New Haven, Conn.: Yale University Press, 1962.

Doppelt, Jerome Edward, The Organization of Mental Abilities, Bureau of Publications, Teachers College, Columbia University, New York, 1950.

Dreger, Ralph M., and Miller, Kent S., "Comparative Psychological Studies of Negroes and Whites in the United States," Psychological Bulletin, 1960, Vol. 57, No. 5, 361-402.

Dunn, L. C., Heredity and Evolution in Human Populations, Harvard University Press, Cambridge, Massachusetts, 1967.

Dunn, L. C., and Dobzhansky, T., Heredity, Race and Society, Rev. ed., New York: New American Library, 1952.

Ebbinghaus, H., Memory: A Contribution of Experimental Psychology, New York, Dover Publication, 1897, 1964.

Edwards, A. C., Experimental Designs in Psychological Research, Revised ed., New York: Holt, Rinehart and Winston, Inc., 1960.

Edwards, Allen J., Individual Mental Testing, Intext Educational Publishers, San Francisco, 1971.

Edwards, A. S., "Intelligence as the Capacity for Variability or Versatility of Responses," Psychological Review, 35, 1928, 198-210.

Edwards, G. F., "Community and Class Realities: The Ordeal of Change," In The Negro American, eds. T. Parsons and K. B. Clark, Boston: Beacon Press, 1966, 280-302.

Eells, Kenneth; Davis, Allison, Havighurst, Robert J., Herrick, Virgil E., Tyler, Ralph W., Intelligence and Cultural Differences, The University of Chicago Press, Chicago and London, 1951.

Elkin, Frederick and Handel, Gerald, The Child and Society: The Process of Socialization, Second Edition, Random House, New York, 1972.

Entwisle, D. R., "Form Class and Children's Word Associations," Journal of Verbal Learning Verbal Behavior, 1966, 5, 558-565.

Eysenck, H. J., "Changing Human Nature," The I.Q. Argument, Illinois, 1971.

Fairchild, H. P., Dictionary of Sociology, New York: Philosophical Library, 1968.

Fantini, Mario D., and Weinstein, Gerald, The Disadvantaged: Challenge to Education, New York, Harper and Row, 1968.

Farr, T. J., "The Intelligence and Achievement of Negro Children," Education, 1931, 51, 491-495.

Ferguson, G. O., Jr., "The Psychology of the Negro: An Experimental Study," Archives of Psychology, No. 36, 1916.

Ford, E. B., Mendelism and Evolution, Methuen and Company Ltd., London, Fifth Edition, 1949.

Frazier, E. F., "Problems and Needs of Negro Children and Youth Resulting from Family Disorganization," Journal of Negro Education, 1950, 19.

Freeman, Frank S., Theory and Practice of Psychological Testing, Revised edition, Henry Holt and Company, New York, 1955.

French, J., and Michael W., Standards for Educational and Psychological Tests and Manuals, Washington, D.C.: American Psychological Association, 1966.

Galton, F., Natural Inheritance, New York: Macmillan, 1894.

Galton, F., Hereditary Genius: An Inquiry into its Laws and Consequences, New York: Macmillan, 1896, 1914.

Galton, F., Inquiries into Human Faculty and its Development, London, J. M. Dent, 1907.

Gardner, G. E., and Aaron, Sadie, "The Childhood and Adolescent Adjustment of Negro Psychiatric Casualties," American Journal Orthopsychiatry, 1946, 16.

Garn, R. M., Human Races, Springfield, Ill.: C. C. Thomas, 1961

Gartn, T. A., Race Psychology: A Study of Racial Mental Differences, New York: McGraw-Hill, 1931.

Gesell, A., The Mental Growth of the Preschool Child, New York: Macmillan, 1925.

Gesell, A., and Amatruda, C., Developmental Diagnosis, 2nd ed., revised and enlarged, New York, Harper, 1947.

Gesell, A., and Thompson, H., The Psychology of Early Growth, New York, The Macmillan Company, 1938.

Gaito, J., "Repeated Measurements Designs and Tests of Null Hypotheses," Educational and Psychological Measurement, 1973, 33, 69-75.

Gilbert, W. S., <u>The Kikado</u>, New York: Modern Library, Random House, 1885.

Ginsberg, Morris, "Essays in Sociology and Social Philosophy," Volume 1 of <u>The Diversity of Morals</u>, ppxxoo-xiv, 1956.

Ginzberg, E., <u>The Middle-Class Negro in the White Man's World</u>, New York: Columbia University Press, 1967.

Gittler, Joseph B., <u>Social Thought Among the Early Greeks</u>, Athens: The University of Georgia Press, 1941.

Glaser, R., "Individuals and Learning: The New Aptitudes," <u>Educational Researcher</u>, 1972, I, 5-13.

Goddard, H. H., <u>Feeblemindedness: Its Causes and Consequences</u>, New York: The Macmillan Company, 1914.

Goddard, H. H., <u>Heredity of Feeblemindedness</u>, Bulletin No. 1, Eugenics Record Office, Cold Spring Harbor, New York, 1911.

Goddard, H. H., "Heredity of Feeblemindedness," Proceedings of the American Philosophical Society, LI, April, 1912.

Goddard, H. H., <u>The Kallikak Family</u>, New York: The Macmillan Company, 1912.

Goddard, H. H., "Two Thousand Normal Children Measured by the Binet Measuring Scale of Intelligence," <u>Pedagogical Seminary</u>, 1910, 17, 387-397.

Goddard, H. H., "Two Thousand Normal Children Measured by the Binet Measuring Scale of Intelligence," <u>Pedagogical Seminary</u>, 1911, 18, 233-259.

Goldberg, M. L., Passow, A. H., and Justman, J., <u>The Effects of Ability Grouping</u>, New York: Teachers College Press, 1966.

Goldfarb, W., "Psychological Privation in Infancy and Subsequent Adjustment," <u>American Journal of Orthopsychiatry</u>, 1945, 15, 247.

Goldfarb, W., "The Effects of Psychological Deprivation in Infancy and Subsequent Stimulation," <u>American Journal of Psychiatry</u>, 1945, 102, 18-33.

Goldfarb, W., "Infant Rearing and Problem Behavior," <u>American Journal of Orthopsychiatry</u>, 1943, 13, 249.

Goodenough, Florence L., <u>Mental Testing</u>, Rinehart and Company, Inc., New York, 1949.

Goodsell, William, "The New Eugenics and Education," <u>The Social Frontier</u>, IV, January 1938, 113-117.

Graham, J. L., "A Quantitative Comparison of Rational Responses of Negro and White College Students," Journal of Social Psychology, 1930, I, 97-121.

Graham, V. T., "Health Studies of Negro Children I. Intelligence Studies of Negro Children in Atlanta, Georgia," Public Health Report, 1926, 41, 2759-2783.

Grambs, J. D., "What Research Says to the Teacher: Understanding Inter-group Relations," revised ed., Washington, National Education Association, 1968.

Guildford, J. P., The Nature of Human Intelligence, New York: McGraw-Hill, 1967.

Gulliksen, Harold, Theory of Mental Tests, John Wiley and Sons, Inc., London, Sydney, 1950.

Haggerty, S., "In Symposium: Intelligence and its Measurement," Journal of Educational Psychology, 1921, 12, 127-133.

Hardin, Garrett, Nature and Man's Fate, New York, New American Library, 1961, c1959.

Havighurst, R. J., and Breese, F. H., "Relation Between Ability and Social Status in a Midwestern Community. III. Primary Mental Abilities," Journal of Educational Psychology, 1947, 38, 241=247.

Havighurst, R. J., Davis, A. A., "A Comparison of the Chicago and Harvard Studies of Social Class Differences in Child Rearing," American Sociological Review, 1955, 20, 438-442.

Havighurst, Robert J., and Levine, Daniel U., Education in Metropolitan Areas, Allyn and Bacon, Inc., Boston, Second edition, 1971.

Havighurst, Robert, and Neugarten, Bernice, Society and Education, Boston: Allyn and Bacon, Inc., 1962.

Herrick, D. J., :A Comparison of Brahman and Panchama Children in South India with each other and with American Children by means of the Goddard Form Board," Journal of Applied Psychology, V, 253-260.

Herrnstein, R. J., "I.Q.," The Atlantic Monthly, September, 1971, 43-64.

Herim, A. W., The Appraisal of Intelligence, National Foundation for Educational Research in England and Wales, 1954, 1970.

Herskovits, M. J., "On the Relation Between Negro-White Mixture and Standing in Intelligence Tests," Pedagogical Seminary, 33, 1926, 30-43.

Hess, R. D., and Shipman, V. C., "Early Experience and the Socialization of Cognitive Modes in Children" Child Development, 1965, 34, 869-886.

Hess, R. D., Shipman, B. C., Brophy, J. E., and Beal, R. M., <u>The Cognitive Environments of Urban Pre-School Children</u>, The Graduate School of Education, University of Chicago, 1968.

Hewitt, A., "A Comparative Study of White and Colored Pupils in a Southern School System," <u>Elementary School Journal</u>, 1930, 31, 111-119.

Hoffman, M. L., and Albizu-Miranda, C., "Middle Class Bias in Personality Testing," Journal of Abnormal and Social Psychology, 1955, 51.

Hollingshead, A. B., "Class Differences in Family Stability," In R. Bendix and S. M. Lipsit (eds.), <u>Class, Status and Power: A Reader in Social Stratification</u>, Glencoe, Ill., Free Press, 1953.

Hollingshead, A. B., <u>Two Factor Index of Social Position</u>, New Haven: Privately Printed, 1957.

Holmes, Samuel J., <u>The Eugenic Predicament</u>, New York, Harcourt, Brace and Company, 1933.

Holmes, Samuel J., <u>Studies in Evolution and Eugenics: The Evolution of Animal Intelligence</u>, New York, H. Holt and Company, 1911.

Holt, John C., <u>How Children Fail</u>, New York, Pitman, 1964.

Holt, John C., <u>How Children Learn</u>, New York, Pitman, 1967.

Horton, Paul B., and Hunt, Chester, L., <u>Sociology</u>, 2nd ed., New York: McGraw-Hill Book Company, 1964.

Hunt, J. McVicker, <u>Intelligence and Experience</u>, The Ronald Press Company, New York, 1961.

Hunt, W. A., "The Relative Incidence of Psychoneurosis Among Negroes," <u>Journal of Consulting Psychology</u>, 1947, 11.

Jencks, C., <u>Inequality</u>, New York: Basic Books, 1972.

Jensen, A., "Another Look at Culture-fair Testing," In J. Hellmuth (ed.), <u>Disadvantaged Child</u>, Vol. 3, New York: Bruner/Mazel, 1970.

Jensen, A. R., "How Much Can We Booster IQ and Scholastic Achievement?" <u>Harvard Educational Review,</u> 39, Winter, 1969.

Irwin, O. C., "Infant Speech: The Effect of Family Occupational Status and of Age on Use of Sound Types," <u>Journal of Speech and Hearing Disorders</u>, 1948, 13, 224-226 (a).

Irwin, O. C., "Infant Speech: The Effects of Family Occupational Status and of Age on Sound Frequency," <u>Journal of Speech and Hearing Disorders</u>, 1948, 13, 320-323 (b).

Johnson, G. E., "Contribution of the Psychology and Pedagogy of Feeble-minded Children," Pedagogical Seminary, Vol. III, No. 2, 246-301.

Johnson, S. T., "Information, Intelligence and Their Relation for First Grade Pupils," Unpublished Master's Thesis, Fish University, 1954.

Johnston, Katherine L., "An English Version of Binet's Test for the Measurement of Intelligence," Report of the British Association for the Advancement of Science, 1910, 80, 806-808.

Johnston, Katherine L., "M. Binet's Method for the Measurement of Intelligence: Some Results," Journal of Experimental Pedagogy, 1911, 1, 24-31.

Kagan, J., "Reflection-Impulsivity and Reading Ability in Primary Grade Children," Child Development, 1965, 36, 609-628.

Kagan, J., "Impulsive and Reflective Children: Significance of Conceptual Tempo," In J. D. Krimboltz (ed.), Learning and the Educational Process, Chicago: Rand McNally, 1965, 133-161.

Kagan, J., "Reflection-Impulsivity: The Generality and Dynamics of Conceptual Tempo," Journal of Abnormal Psychology, 1966, 71, 17-24.

Kagan, J., and Moss, H. A., Birth to Maturity: A Study in Psychological Development, New York: Wiley, 1962.

Kagan, J. S., and Moss, H. A., "Parental Correlates of Child IQ and Height: A Cross-Validation of the Berkeley Growth Study Results," Child Development, 30, 1959, 325-332.

Katz, J. J., "Recent Issues in Semantic Theory," Foundations Language, 1967, 3, 124-194.

Kelley, J., "Psychophysical Tests of Normal and Abnormal Children," In Pintner, R., Intelligence Testing, Henry Holt and Company, New York, 1931.

Kennedy, Daniel B., Resocialization: An American Experiment, Behavioral Publications, New York, 1973.

Kennedy, W. A., Van de Riet, V., and White, J. C., "A Normative Sample of Intelligence and Achievement of Negro Elementary School Children in the Southeastern United States," Monograms of Society Research on Child Development, 1963, 28, 112.

Kephart, W. M., "The Negro Offender: An Urban Research Project," American Journal of Sociology, 1954, 60.

Kerckhoff, Alan C., Socialization and Social Class, Prentice-Hall, Inc., Englewood Cliffs, N.J., 1972.

Kirk, R. E., Experimental Design: Procedures for the Behavioral Sciences, Brooks/Cole Publishing Company, California, 1968.

Klineberg, Otto, "An Experimental Study of Speed and Other Factors in 'Racial' Differences," Archives of Psychology, 15, No. 93, 1928.

Klineberg, Otto, Race Differences, Harper and Brothers Publishers, New York and London, 1935.

Koch, H. L., and Simmons, R., "A Study of the Test-Performance of American Mexican and Negro Children," Psychological Monograms, 1926, 35, 116.

Labov, William, "Academic Ignorance and Black Intelligence," The Atlantic Monthly, September, 1971, 59-67.

Labov, W., "The Logic of Nonstandard English," In F. Williams (ed.), Language and Poverty, Chicago: Markham, 1970, 153-189.

Lacy, L. D., "Relative Intelligence of White and Colored Children," Elementary School Journal, 1926, 26, 542-546.

Lee, E. S., and Lee, Anne S., "The Differential Fertility of the American Negro," American Sociological Review, 1952, 17.

Lesser, G., Fifer, G., D., "Mental Abilities of Children from Different Social-Class and Cultural Groups," Monograph of the Society for Research in Child Development, 1965, 30, 1-115.

Levy, D. M., Maternal Overprotection, New York: Columbia University Press, 1943.

Lindquist, E. F., Design and Analysis of Experiments in Psychology and Education, Boston: Houghton Miffin Company, 1953.

Loades, H. R., and Rich, S. G., "Binet Tests on South African Natives -- Zulus," Pedagogical Seminary, 1917, XXIV, 373-383.

Lorge, I., Third Mental Measurement Yearbook, O. K. Buros, edition, New Brunswick, N.J.: Rutgers University Press, 1949.

Ludmerer, Kenneth M., Genetics and American Society, Baltimore, John Hopkins University Press, 1972.

McCandless, B. R., Children: Behavior and Development, New York: Holt, Rinehart and Winston, 1967.

McCandless, B. R., and Evans, E. B., Children and Youth: Psychosocial Development, The Dryden Press, Hinsdale, Illinois, 1973.

McDavid, J. W., "Personality and Situational Determinants of Conformity," Journal of Abnormal and Social Psychology, 1959, 58, 241-246.

McDavid, J. W., and Harari, H., Social Psychology: Individuals, Groups, Societies, New York: Harper and Row, 1968.

McDavid, J. W., and Harari, H., Psychology and Social Behavior, Harper and Row, 1974.

McGraw, M. B., "A Comparative Study of a Group of Southern White and Negro Infants," Genetic Psychological Monograms, 1931, 10, 1-105.

McGraw, M. B., "Maturation of Behavior," in L. Carmichael (ed.), Manual of Child Psychology, New York: Wiley, 1946, 332-369.

McKinley, Donald Gilbert, Social Class and Family Life, Collier-Macmillan Limited, London, 1964.

Martin, A. L., "Experiments with Binet-Simon Test Upon African Colored Children, Chiefly Kaffus," Training School Bulletin, 1915, 12.

Mead, Margaret, New Lives for Old, New York, Morrow, 1928, 1966.

Menacker, Julius and Pollack, Erwin, Emerging Educational Issues, Little, Brown and Company, Boston, 1974.

Mitchell, D., Schools and Classes for Exceptional Children, Cleveland Education Survey, 1929.

Montagu, A., Race and IQ, Oxford University Press, London, 1975.

Montagu, M. F. A., "Intelligence of Northern Negroes and Southern Whites in the First World War," American Journal of Psychology, 1945, 58, 161-188.

Moore, 1942. See Shuey, 1966.

Moore, B., Hoch, E., Casebook on Ethical Standards of Psychologists, Washington, D.C.: American Psychological Association, 1967.

Moses, E. R., "Differentials in Crime Rates Between Negroes and Whites, Based on Comparisons of Four Socio-economically equated areas," American Sociological Review, 1947, 12.

Moynihan, D. P., The Negro Family: The Case for National Action, Washington, D.C.: Office of Policy Planning and Research, U.S. Department of Labor.

Mussen, Paul H., Carmichael's Manual of Child Psychology, Third edition, Volumes 1 and 2, John Wiley and Sons, Inc., New York, 1970.

Nissen, H. W., Machover, S., and Kinder, E. F., "A Study of Performance Tests Given to a Group of Native African Negro Children," British Journal of Psychology, V. 25, 1934-35, 308-355.

Pasamanick, B. A., "Comparative Study of the Behavioral Development of Negro Infants," Journal of Genetic Psychology, 69, 1946, 2-44.

Oliver, Richard, "The Musical Talent of Natives of East Africa," British Journal of Psychology, V. 22, 1931-32, 333-343.

Oakland, T., and Phillips, B. N., Assessing Minority Group Children: A Special Issue of the Journal of School Psychology, Behavioral Publications, New York, 1973.

Patrick, J. R., and Sims, W. M., "Personality Differences Between Negro and White College Students, North and South," Journal of Abnormal and Social Psychology, 1934, 29, 181-201.

Perring, L. F., "A Study of the Comparative Retardation of Negro and White Pupils in a Philadelphia School," Psychological Clinic, 1915, 9.

Peterson, J., Early Conceptions and Tests of Intelligence, Yonkers-on-Hudson, New York, World Book, 1925.

Peterson, J., "In Symposium: Intelligence and its Measurement," Journal of Educational Psychology, 1921, 12, 127-133.

Peterson, J., "The Comparative Abilities of White and Negro Children," Comp. Psychological Monograms, 1923, I, No. 5, 141.

Pettitt, George A., Prisoners of Culture, Charles Scriber's Sons, New York, 1970.

Phillips, B. A., "The Binet Tests Applied to Colored Children," Psychological Clinic, 1914, 8, 190-196.

Piaget, Jean, Psychology and Epistomeology: Toward A Theory of Knowledge, translated by Arnold Rosin, The Viking Press, New York, 1970(a).

Piaget, Jean, Science of Education and The Psychology of the Child, translated by Coltman, Orion Press, New York, 1970(b).

Piaget, Jean, Biology and Knowledge, translated by Beatrix, Walsh, Chicago, University of Chicago Press, 1971.

Piaget, J., and Inhelder, B., The Growth of Logical Thinking From Childhood to Adolescence, translated by Parsons and Milgram, New York, Basic Books, 1958.

Piaget, J., and Inhelder, B., Memory and Intelligence, translated by Pomerans, New York, Basic Books, 1973.

Piaget, J., and Inhelder B., The Psychology of the Child, translated by Weaver, New York, Basic Books, 1969(a).

Piaget, J., and Inhelder, B., The Psychology of Intelligence, translated by Berlyne, London, Routledge and Paul, 1951.

Piaget, J., and Inhelder, B., Three Theories of Development, New York, Harper and Row, 1969(b).

Pickens, Donald K., Eugenics and the Progressives, Vanderbilt University Press, 1968.

Pieron, H., "The Problem of Intelligence," Pedagogical Seminary, 33, 1931, 50-60.

Pintner, R., "An Empirical View of Intelligence," Journal of Educational Psychology, 17, 1926, 608-616.

Pintner, R., Intelligence Testing, Henry Holt and Company, New York, 1931.

Polgan, Steven, "Biculturation of Mesquakie Teenage Boys," American Anthropologist, 62, 1960, 217-235.

Pollack, O., "A Statistical Investigation of the Cuminality of Old Age," Journal of Clinical Psychopathology, 1944, 5.

Pollack, Robert H., and Brenner, Margaret, W., "The Experimental Psychology of Alfred Binet," Springer Publishing Company, Inc., New York City, 1969.

Porteus, S. D., "Mental Tests with Delinquent and Australian Aboriginal Children," Psychological Review, XXIV, 1917, 33-42.

Porteus, S. D., "Race and Social Differences in Performance Tests," Genetic Psychology Monograms, No. 8, 1930.

Putnam, G. N., and O'Hern, E., "The Status Significance of an Isolated Urban Dialect," Language Dissertation, No. 53, Language, 1955, 31 (4), Whole Part 2.

Reese, Hayne W., and Lipsitt, Lewis, P., Experimental Child Psychology, Academic Press, New York, 1970.

Reissman, D., The Culturally Deprived Child, New York, Harper, 1962.

Rhoads, T. F., Rapoport, M., Kennedy, R., and Stokes, J., Jr., "Studies on the Growth and Development of Male Children Receiving Evaporated Milk II. Physical Growth, Dentition and Intelligence of White and Negro Children Through the First Years as Influenced by Vitam Supplements," Journal of Pediatrics, 1945, 26, 415-454.

Ripley, H. S., and Wolf, S., "Mental Illness Among Negro Troops Overseas," American Journal of Psychiatry, 1947, 103.

Robson, G. M., "Social Factors in Mental Retardation," British Journal of Psychology, V. 22, 1931-32, 118-136.

Roucek, Joseph S., in Dictionary of Socialogy, ed. by Henry Pratt. Fairchild, Totowa: Littlefield, Adams and Company, 1968.

Rouse, W. H. D., Great Dialogues of Plato, New American Library, New York, 1956.

Rowntree, L. G., "The Unfit: How to Exclude Them," <u>Psychosomatic Med.</u>, 1943, 5.

Samuda, Ronald J., <u>Psychological Testing of American Minorities</u>; <u>Issues and Consequences</u>, Dobb, Mean and Company, New York, 1975.

Sarason, S. B., and Gladwin, T., "Psychological and Cultural Problems in Mental Subnormality: A Review of Research," <u>Genetic Psychology Monograms</u>, 1958, 57, 3-289.

Scheffe, H., <u>The Analysis of Variance</u>, John Wiley and Sons, Inc., London, 1959.

Sharp, S. E., "Individual Psychology: A Study in Psychological Method," <u>American Journal of Psychology</u>, Vol. X, 1899, 329-391.

Sherman, Mandel, <u>Intelligence and its Deviations</u>, The Ronald Press Company New York, 1945.

Shuey, A., <u>The Testing of Negro Intelligence</u>, Lynchburg, Va., J. P. Bell, 1958.

Shuey, A., <u>The Testing of Negro Intelligence</u>, 2nd ed., New York, Social Science Press, 1966.

Simpson, Benjamin R., <u>Correlations of Mental Abilities</u>, Teachers College, Columbia University, New York City, 1912, AMS edition, 1972.

Sims, V. M., <u>Social Class Identification Occupational Rating Scale</u>, New York: Harcourt, Bruce and World, 1952.

Skeels, H. M., "Adult Status of Children with Contracting Early Life Experiences," <u>Monograms of Social Research in Child Development</u>, 1966, 31, No. 3, Serial No. 105.

Slakter, M. J., <u>Statistical Inference for Educational Researchers</u>, Addison-Wesley Publishing Co., Reading Massachusetts, 1972.

Sorokin, P., <u>Fads and Foibles in Modern Sociology</u>, Chicago, Henry Regnery Company, 1956, 3-20.

Spiker, C. C., and McCandless, B. R., "The Concept of Intelligence and the Philosophy of Science," <u>Psychological Review</u>, 1954, 61, 255-266.

Stern, W., <u>The Psychological Methods of Testing Intelligence</u>, Translated by Whipple, Baltimore, 1914.

Steward, W. A., "Creole Language in the Caribbean," in <u>Study of the Role of Second Languages in Asia, Africa and Latin America</u>, ed. by Frank Rice, Washington, D.C.: Center for Applied Linguistics, 1962.

Steward, W. A., <u>Non-Standard Speech and the Teaching of English</u>, Washington, D.C.: Center for Applied Linguistics, 1964.

Steward, W. A., "Urban Negro Speech: Socialization Factors Affecting English Teaching," in <u>Social Dialects and Language Learning</u>, ed. by Roger W. Shuy, Champlain, Ill.: National Council of Teachers of English, 1965.

Steward, W. A., "Observations on the Problems of Defining Negro Dialect," in <u>Conference on the Language Component in the Training of Teachers of English and Reading: Views and Problems</u>, Washington, D.C.: Center for Applied Linguistics and the National Council of Teachers of English, 1966.

Steward, W. A., "Nonstandard Speech Patterns," in <u>Baltimore Bulletin of Education</u>, 43, 1967, 52-65.

Steward, W. A., "On the use of Negro Dialect in the Teaching of Reading," in <u>Teaching Black Children to Read</u>, ed. by Joan Baratz and Roger Shuy, Washington, D.C.: Center for Applied Linguistics, 1969.

Strong, A. C., "Three Hundred Fifty White and Colored Children Measured by Binet-Simon Measuring Scale of Intelligence: A Comparative Study," <u>Pedagogical Seminary</u>, 1913, 20, 485-515.

Sunne, D., "A Comparative Study of White and Negro Children," <u>Journal of Applied Psychology</u>, 1917, I, 71-83.

Sunne, D., "Comparison of White and Negro Children by the Terman and Yerkes Bridges Revisions of the Binet Tests," <u>Journal of Comparative Psychology</u>, 1925, 5, 209-219.

Sunne, D., "Comparison of White and Negro Children in Verbal and Non-verbal Tests," <u>School and Sociology</u>, 1924, 19, 469-472.

Suttles, Gerald D., <u>The Social Order of the Slum</u>, The University of Chicago Press, Chicago, 1968.

Suttles, Gerald D., <u>The Social Construction of Communities</u>, The University of Chicago Press, Chicago, 1972.

Terman, L. M., "Genius and Stupidity: A Study of Some of the Intellectual Processes of Seven 'Bright' and seven 'Stupid' Boys," <u>Pedagogical Seminary</u>, 1906, 13, 307-373.

Terman, L. M., "In Symposium: Intelligence and its Measurement," <u>Journal of Educational Psychology</u>, 1921, 12, 127-133.

Terman, L. M., and Childs, H. G., "Tentative Revision and Extension of the Binet and Simon Measuring Scale of Intelligence," <u>Journal of Educational Psychology</u>, 1912, 3, 61-74, 133-143, 198-208, 277-289.

Thorndike, R., "Concepts of Culture-Fairness," <u>Journal of Educational Psychology</u>, 1971, 8, 63-70.

Thorndike, R. L., "In Symposium: Intelligence and its Measurement," <u>Journal of Educational Psychology</u>, 1921, 12, 127-133.

Thorndike, R. L., and Hagen, E., <u>Measurement and Evaluation in Psychology</u> <u>and Education</u>, John Wiley and Sons, Inc., New York, 1969.

Thurstone, L. L., <u>The Nature of Intelligence</u>, Greenwood Press, Westport, Connecticut, 1924, reprint 1973.

Thurstone, L. L., and Thurstone, J., <u>Primary Mental Abilities</u>, Chicago, Ill., The University of Chicago Press, 1938.

Tornlinson, H., "Differences Between Pre-School Negro Children and Their Older Siblings on the Stanford-Binet Scales," <u>Journal of Negro</u> <u>Education</u>, 1944, 13, 474-479.

Trabue, M. R., "Intelligence of Negro Recruits," <u>National History</u>, 1919, 19, 680-685.

Tyler, Leona E., Intelligence: <u>Some Recurring Issues</u>, Van Nostrand Reinhold Company, New York, 1969.

Valentine, C. A., "A Plan for Positive Discrimination in Employment," <u>Realities</u>, 1966, 1(2), 6-8.

Valentine, C. A., <u>Empowering the Poor to end Poverty: A Proposal</u>, St. Louis: Sunshine Press, 1967.

Valentine, C. A., <u>Culture and Poverty: Critique and Counterproposal</u>, Chicago: University of Chicago Press, 1968.

Valentine, C. A., "Deficit, Difference, and Bicultural Models of Afro-American Behavior," <u>Harvard Educational Review</u>, 1971, 41, 137-157.

Valentine, C. A., and Valentine, B. L., "Making the Scene; Digging the Action, and Telling it Like it is: Anthropologists at Work in a Dark Ghetto," in <u>Afro-American Anthropology: Contemporary Perspectives</u>, ed. by Norman Whitten and John Szwed, New York: Free Press, 1971.

Valentine, C. A., "Models and Muddles Concerning Culture and Inequality: A Reply to Critics," <u>Harvard Educational Review</u>, 42, 1972, 1, 97-108.

Valien, P., and Vaughn, Ruth E., "Birth Control Attitudes and Practices of Negro Mothers," <u>Sociological Social Research</u>, 1951, 35.

Warner, W. L., Meeher, M., and Eels, K., <u>Social Class in America</u>, Chicago: Science Research Associates, 1949.

Warren, Roland, L., <u>The Community in America</u>, Rand McNally and Company, Second Edition, Chicago, 1972.

Wechsler, D., "A Study of the Subtests of the Bellevue Intelligence Scale in Borderline and Mental Defective Cases," <u>American Journal of Mental</u> <u>Deficiency</u>, Vol. 45, 1941.

Wechsler, D., _The Measurement of Adult Intelligence_, 3rd ed., Baltimore: Williams and Wilkins, 1944.

Wechsler, D., _Wechsler Bellevue Intelligence Scale Form II_, New York: Psychological Corporation, 1946.

Wechsler, D., _Manual for the Wechsler Intelligence Scale for Children_, New York: The Psychological Corporation, 1949.

Wells, F. L., _Mental Tests in Clinical Practice_, Yonkers-on-Hudson, New York, World Book Company, 1927.

Whipple, G. M., _Manual of Mental and Physical Tests_, Baltimore: Warwick and York, 1910.

Winer, B. J., _Statistical Principles in Experimental Design_, New York: McGraw-Hill Book Company, 1962.

Witmer, L., "Clinical Psychology," _Psychological Clinic_, Vol. I, No. 1, 1930, 1-9.

Woisika, P. H., "An Evaluation of the Dark Test," _American Internal Medicine_, 1944, 21.

Wolfe, R. M., "The Identification and Measurement of Environmental Process Variables Related to Intelligence," Unpublished Dissertation, University of Chicago, 1964.

Woodworth, R. S., "The Comparative Psychology of Races," _Psychological Bulletin_, 1916, 13, 388.

Yerkes, Robert M., Bridges, J. W., and Hardwick, R. S., _A Point Scale for Measuring Mental Ability_, Baltimore: Warwick and York, 1965.

Yerkes, Robert M., _Army Mental Tests_, New York, H. Holt and Company, 1920.

Yerkes, Robert M., _The New World of Science_, Freeport, New York, Books for Libraries Press, 1969, c1920.

Young, F. M. and Bright, H. A., "Results of Testing 81 Negro Rural Juveniles with the Wechsler Intelligence Scale for Children" _Journal of Social Psychology_, 1954, 39, 219-226.

Young, Kimball, _Sociology: A Study of Society and Culture_, 2nd ed., New York: American Book Company, 1949.

Zach, Lillian, "The IQ Debate," _Today's Education_, September, 1972.